Dedication

To Millie Wyckoff and Robert Unell,
for their love and empathy that inspire our joy,
humor, hope, trust, confidence, and contentment,
and for giving meaning and purpose
to each day of our lives.

Contents

Section VIII: Sleeping

Section IX: Growing Up

Section X: Health

Preface

For the past twenty years, we've traveled the country teaching parents how to discipline their children without shouting or spanking, how to develop their children's inborn traits, and how to learn to be teaching parents. Along the way, thousands of parents, grandparents, teachers, and babysitters have asked us to provide easy-to-use strategies to help them with the everyday problem of motivating their children to cooperate.

We've seen firsthand the need for this book in today's hurried, worried world that's focused so intently on instant gratification. With the touch of a button, we change channels to get the latest news. After a few minutes in the microwave, we have breakfast, lunch, or dinner. With a flick of the wrist, we play a new computer game or schedule our day on a pop-up screen.

It's not surprising, then, that we see more and more parents expecting immediate compliance from their children. And when children don't instantly respond, we see parents resorting to nagging, shaming, guilt-tripping, bribing, and threatening their children with spanking or some other form of violence. While these strategies may lead children to do what they're told, they ultimately break down children's wills and create anger and resentment. Children cooperate because they're *afraid not* to, not because they *want* to. We describe these hurtful strategies in this book to ensure that well-intentioned parents understand how damaging they are.

In contrast, the positive strategies described in this book not only teach parents how to motivate their children to cooperate, they also help children learn to be empathetic team players, to tolerate frustration, to make responsible decisions, and to delay gratification. These strategies also help build positive parent-child relationships based on trust and unconditional love.

Research has shown that parents face the problem of motivating their children to cooperate hundreds of times each day![1] Each of these situations is an opportunity for parents to build their patience, empathy, tolerance, and negotiating skills, and to develop the same skills in their children. In addition, these situations give parents chances to encourage their little ones' budding independence, to respect their children's need to control their world, and to appreciate the developmental miracle of growing from a baby to a young child. We invite you to keep this book close at hand. In those challenging moments with your child, it'll help you choose constructive thoughts, actions, and words. Your child is listening!

Careful the things you say; children will listen.
Careful the things you do; children will see and learn.
Children may not obey, but children will listen.
Children will look to you for which way to turn, to learn what to be.
Careful before you say, "listen to me"; children will listen!
—"Children Will Listen" by Stephen Sondheim, from *Into the Woods*

Acknowledgments

Our heartfelt thanks to all the toddlers and preschoolers and their dedicated parents and teachers who, knowingly and unknowingly, reminded us of the essence of our message. Particular thanks to the parents of the Christ Episcopal Church Parenting Group, the parents of Temple B'nai Jehudah preschool, Beth Shalom preschool, Parents as Teachers, and the thousands of parents and teachers who have shared their personal lives with us.

Our respect and appreciation to our teachers of lessons in biology, psychology, medicine, and spirituality that have informed this book: Martin E. P. Seligman, PhD; Norman Cousins; Daniel Goleman, PhD; Norman Vincent Peale; Daniel Amen, MD; Steven Pinker, PhD; Barbara Fredrickson, PhD; Jonathan Haidt, PhD; Deepak Chopra, MD; Richard Carlson; Andrew Weil, MD; David Simon, MD; Michael Meyerhoff, EdD; Marguerite Kelly; Amie Jew, MD; Jennifer Bingham, RN; James Coster, MD; Al Buehler; Rachel Schanberg; Carol Fabian, MD; Peter Yarrow; and Mark Weiss.

We are grateful to our editor, Joseph Gredler, for his belief in the virtues of respect and kindness, and his demonstration of those virtues in his work with us. We also appreciate Beth Vesel and Bruce Lansky for their dedication and insight along our literary journey together.

And, of course, our thanks to our beloved children for starting this journey for us: Amy Elizabeth Unell, Justin Alex Unell, Christopher Britton Wyckoff, and Allison Leigh Wyckoff.

Introduction

You hold the key to helping your child cooperate when you remember this important equation: ability + motivation = performance. Human beings of all ages must not only be physically and intellectually *able* to do what they're asked, they must be *willing* to do so. For example, in order for your child to cooperate with your request to get dressed, he must know how to put on his clothes, and he needs a compelling reason to do so.

Herein lies the parenting problem: What's important to you may not be important to him. You may want him to get dressed so you can take him to daycare and get to work on time, but he may want to keep playing with his toys and has no sense of time at all. Your job is twofold: First, determine whether he can get dressed by himself, then give him a reason to *want* to do so.

Teaching your child to cooperate takes time and patience, but the benefits last a lifetime. By following the helpful techniques described in this book (and by avoiding the harmful ones), you can build a loving relationship with your child, teach him the value of teamwork, and increase his ability to delay gratification and tolerate frustration. You can also help your toddler or preschooler learn to express his feelings, empathize with others, and make responsible decisions. These skills are best learned at this stage of development, and they're best taught by your child's first and most important teacher—you.

Why Young Children Say No

Toddlers and preschoolers live in a self-centered world. They want to do *what* they want to do *when* they want to do it. In fact, it's developmentally appropriate for them to behave this way. They also like consistency and predictability. Therefore, they say no in order to avoid the unknown ("I don't wanna get on the airplane!"), to avoid change ("I don't wanna go to a new preschool!"), to avoid failure ("I don't wanna practice piano!"), and to avoid loss of control ("I don't wanna go to daycare!").

In addition, parents often unwittingly encourage uncooperative behavior by ignoring their children when they cooperate and by paying lots of attention when they don't. Children quickly learn that *not* cooperating is an easy way to get their parents' attention. Finally, young children don't usually see the "big picture" parents have in mind when making their requests. Young children have no sense of time, so they don't understand the urgency parents feel in many situations.

Five Important Questions

Before reacting negatively when your child says no, ask yourself these five important questions.

How would I feel if I were my child? Considering your child's point of view is the first step toward finding ways to motivate him to cooperate. Is he tired? Is he having a great time playing with his blocks? Is he watching his favorite show? Is he afraid of something you're asking him to do? Once you understand *his* agenda, you can help him meet yours.

What is my child capable of doing? Are your expectations too high? Is your child physically able to do what you're asking him to do? Can he hear you okay? Can he understand the words you're using? Remember, each child is unique and develops on his own timetable. Consult your healthcare provider if you're concerned about your child's developmental progress.

Have I taught my child what I'm asking him to do? Have you practiced each step to make sure he understands what to do? If not, spend time teaching him how to brush his teeth, for example, before asking him to do so. You may have to practice many times before he masters the skill. Patience is the key!

How many directions can my child follow? If you ask your child to get dressed, turn off the TV, and put away his toys, will he remember to do each thing? Can he follow your directions without getting distracted? If not, test your child's ability to follow directions. After he shows you that he can follow one direction, try two and eventually three at a time.

Am I being a good role model for my child? Has your child ever watched you brush your teeth? Wash your hands? Use your napkin? Wear your seat belt? If not, remember that your child is always watching your example. Practice what you teach!

Harmful Ways to Motivate Children

It's normal for parents to get irritated when their children don't cooperate. Irritation often leads to nagging ("How many times do I have to tell you?"), labeling ("You're so lazy!"), begging ("Do it for Mommy!"), blaming ("Don't make me late again!"), or shaming ("I'm so disappointed in you!"). When these strategies don't work, parents may opt for bribing ("If you put your shoes on, I'll give you some candy.") or, as a last resort, threatening ("If you don't get your shoes on, I'll spank you!").

These techniques may seem justifiable when parents tell themselves that their child's lack of cooperation is an act of defiance. Parents may fear that their child will never listen to them, never be able to get along with others, and never learn to follow directions in school. Their own parents may have nagged, bribed, or threatened them for not following directions, and these responses may come naturally when they're backed into a corner by a child who refuses to cooperate. In addition, parents may become angry or embarrassed because they think their child is making them look like bad parents.

This irrational self-talk stems from parents' frightening realization that they don't have control over their child's behavior. They tell themselves that they *must* control their child, or dire consequences will result. Getting angry is a sign that parents need to change their self-talk. Research has shown that rational self-talk can override irrational responses to the "dangers" parents perceive in their child's behavior.[2] Believing that their child is defiant, for example, may push parents to blame, shame, label, or punish him as an attempt to control his defiance. On the other hand, telling themselves that their child's behavior is developmentally appropriate lets parents reframe the situation as a teachable moment. It gives them a chance to work *with* their child rather than against him.

Nothing positive results from nagging, bribing, or threatening a child. He may do what he's asked out of fear, guilt, or shame, but he won't learn the skills necessary to get along in the world as a responsible, self-sufficient, considerate human being. He'll learn just the opposite: how to intimidate others to get them to do what he wants.

Helpful Ways to Motivate Children

Children's natural empathy needs a loving, nurturing environment in which to emerge and thrive. Therefore, parents need to become empathetic, teaching parents who work with their child to follow the rules they've established. Children learn to care for others by being cared for themselves, and they learn to respect others by being respected themselves. Parents can build their child's trust by helping him learn to make decisions, follow the rules, and accept the consequences of his choices. The positive techniques described below will help parents model patience and self-control as they deal with the daily challenges of motivating their child from no to yes.

Empathize. Show your child that you empathize with his concerns. This validates him and tells him that you respect his opinions, which in turn motivates him to cooperate as part of your team. If you repeatedly scold, find fault, complain, blame, shame, label, and guilt-trip your child, he'll tune you out and learn to use these hurtful tactics on other people.

Make a deal using Grandma's Rule. Grandma's Rule says, "When you've done what I've asked you to do, then you're free to do what you want to do." This peaceful solution to parent-child conflicts teaches your child the value of meeting his responsibilities before doing what he wants. It gives him practice in delaying gratification and tolerating frustration. It helps him develop the internal motivation to get his work done before enjoying his fun. The ultimate benefit of Grandma's Rule is teaching your child the win-win, team approach to meeting everyone's agenda.

Bribery, on the other hand, tells your child, "If you do what I ask, then I'll give you a special prize." It teaches him to hold out for a tangible payoff before cooperating. Once he learns that his cooperation can be bought and sold on the open market, his motivation remains external and totally dependent on the size of the payoff he can receive.

Teach by giving choices. When you give your child choices, he practices his decision-making skills. For example, you might say, "You can play nicely with your sister, or you can play by yourself. You choose." This motivates him to play nicely with his sister in order to remain in her company (something he dearly wants to do).

On the other hand, intimidating your child by threatening to punish him when he doesn't listen tells him that he has no choice in the matter. Because he hasn't been given any say in what happens, his anger, resentment, and reluctance to cooperate will *increase*—the opposite of what you want. Threats lead to fear, and fear motivates your child to escape or rebel rather than cooperate.

Threats also put you in a difficult position. If your child doesn't comply, you're forced to follow through with a punishment that damages your child and your relationship with him; if you don't follow through, your credibility is destroyed. When your child discovers that your threat was empty, he'll no longer believe that you mean what you say. He'll replace his fear of punishment with a fear that nothing is as it seems. It's best to avoid these consequences by avoiding threats.

Using This Book

Each chapter is designed to help you meet both your short-term goal (getting your child to do what you ask) and your long-term goals (teaching him to cope with frustration, delay gratification, express his feelings, empathize with others, make decisions, and be a team player).

Chapter titles reflect common requests made by parents, and common reactions from toddlers and preschoolers. Each chapter title is followed by a brief overview of the psychological and developmental circumstances surrounding the situation.

The "Helpful Hints" sections include tips that encourage cooperation and improve your chances of successfully motivating your child to listen, follow directions, and do what you ask.

The "Self-Talk" sections include the words you say (or think) to yourself that determine your attitude toward events. Self-talk is that little voice in your head that labels an event as either an insurmountable problem or an opportunity to help your child learn an important skill. Remember, all events are neutral; you make them negative or positive based on what you think about them.

It's important to think about your attitude toward your child's behavior *first*, because your attitude influences how you'll respond. For example, when you view your child's refusal to cooperate as an act of defiance, you're likely to respond negatively. When you view your child's resistance as a teachable moment, you're likely to respond reasonably and responsibly.

The "Talking to Your Child" sections include the words you say to your child to motivate him to cooperate. As in the "Self-Talk" sections, it's important to look at what *not* to say—and why—as well as what to say. You should avoid using the "Don't Say" scripts because they motivate through fear, guilt, or shame. On the other hand, we encourage you to adopt the "Say" scripts because they motivate through respect, empathy, kindness, and unconditional love.

SECTION I
GOING PLACES

The way is long—let us go together. The way is difficult—let us help each other. The way is joyful—let us share it. The way is ours alone—let us go in love.

—*Joyce Hunter*

Chapter One

"It's Time to Go Now."
"No! I Don't Wanna Go Now!"

The coffee is comforting, the conversation is pleasant, and the last thing you want to do is leave your happy lunch hour. That's how your three-year-old feels when she protests leaving the park or a friend's house. Instead of expecting her to cooperate immediately, give her time to shift gears by starting the goodbye process several minutes before you need to whisk her away. This will help her adjust to a world that doesn't always run according to her schedule.

Helpful Hints

- ✋ Explain your departure routine before going places with your child, so she knows what to expect. For example, say, "I'll tell you five minutes before it's time to go. That way you'll have plenty of time to say goodbye to your friends, put on your coat, and get ready to leave."

- ✋ As you're preparing to leave, help your child complete necessary tasks such as putting on her coat, putting away toys, using the bathroom, and so on.

- ✋ Your comments and attitude are contagious, so keep them positive to encourage cooperation when it's time to go.

Self-Talk

Don't tell yourself,
"I can't stand my child's defiance."
Telling yourself you can't stand something evokes feelings of helplessness and hopelessness, and it closes the door to finding creative solutions to problems. Telling yourself you can't tolerate her defiance also may cause you to become angry and frustrated, which may further discourage her cooperation.

Instead, tell yourself,

**"I can handle my child's need to be her
own person and make her own decisions."**

You're free to choose how to react to your child's behavior. Telling yourself you *can* do something boosts your confidence, and the resulting positive emotions open your mind to various solutions. When you're feeling hopeful and empathetic, your interactions with your child will be positive and supportive, which is crucial in motivating her to cooperate.

Don't tell yourself,

"These people must think I'm an incompetent parent."

When you start imagining that people think you're a bad parent, you're likely to start believing it, which will prevent you from finding constructive ways to manage your child's behavior. Don't worry about what you don't know and can't control, such as the thoughts of those around you.

Instead, tell yourself,

"My goal isn't to impress other people."

Keep in mind the long-term goal of helping your child learn to cooperate by handling change and frustration. This will help you frame a more effective response.

Don't tell yourself,

**"She makes me so mad! I'm afraid of what
I might do to her if she doesn't get ready to leave NOW!"**

Your child's behavior can't make you angry; only what you *think* about your child's behavior can do that. If you demand something you can't control, such as your child's cooperation, you're likely to become angry. Only she can choose to follow directions, so help her learn to make that decision.

Instead, tell yourself,

**"I'm not going to demand that my child cooperate.
That only makes me angry."**

Choosing to get angry blocks your ability to solve problems empathetically. Thinking that you'd *like* her to cooperate opens your mind to creative ways to encourage her to do so.

Talking to Your Child

Don't whine. Don't say,
> *"Why can't you ever do what I say?*
> *No matter how long we stay, it's never enough for you!"*

This attack suggests that your child has a built-in character flaw rather than a developmentally appropriate desire to follow her own agenda.

Instead, give directions. Say,
> *"It's going to be time to go in five minutes.*
> *Let's start picking things up now."*

Pleasantly reminding your child of the departure routine lets her finish her activities and prepare for the change that's about to take place.

Don't threaten. Don't say,
> *"Don't you say no to me, young lady!*
> *If you're not careful, you'll get a spanking!"*

Threatening to physically hurt your child only tells her that you're bigger and stronger and that violence is an acceptable way of getting what you want from those who are smaller and weaker.

Instead, use empathy. Say,
> *"I understand that you don't want to leave now,*
> *but sometimes we have to do things we don't like."*

Putting yourself in your child's shoes validates her feelings and helps elicit her cooperation. It also lets you keep your goals in mind: staying on schedule and teaching her to cope with disappointment.

Don't tattle. Don't say,
> *"Wait until I tell your father how uncooperative you're being.*
> *He won't be happy with you at all."*

Tattling on your child teaches her that she should fear her parents and that she can achieve cooperation by threatening to make someone mad. It also models how to tattle on others. If you tell your child, "Your father won't be happy with you," you teach her that her parents' love is conditional. Saying that she's being uncooperative tells her that what she does defines who she is. These messages undermine your relationship with your child.

Instead, play a game. Say,

> *"I'm going to count to ten. Let's see if you can get your jacket on before I get there. Ready? One, two...."*

Defuse a potentially explosive situation by playing a fun-loving game. This will shift your child's focus from resistance to competition and get her moving in the direction you want. If your child doesn't finish by the count of ten, say, "I'm sorry you didn't make it in time. I'll help you put your coat on now. When we get home, we'll practice playing the game. Then you'll be able to do what I ask by the time I finish counting."

Don't bribe. Don't say,

> *"Sweetheart, if you come with me now, we'll stop by the store and get you a treat."*

Bribing your child only encourages her to refuse to cooperate until she can get a promise of a material reward. Using food as the reward further complicates the situation by linking food with your approval, which can set the stage for eating disorders or other food-related problems.

Instead, use a positive consequence. Say,

> *"Getting ready to go when it's time means that we can come back soon."*

This tells your child that her cooperation is the key to getting to do what she wants in the future, an important first step in teaching her to delay gratification and tolerate temporary frustration.

Chapter Two

"Please Get in the Car."
"No! I Don't Wanna Get in the Car!"

Is your wriggly four-year-old refusing to get in the car because he doesn't want to wear his seat belt? Because he's tired or hungry? Because he wants to stay home and play? Maybe he's afraid his tummy will hurt, as it often does while cruising along the highway. Ask your child what he's feeling so you can resolve the issue and reassure yourselves that the journey ahead will be a joy ride for all.

Helpful Hints

✋ Whenever possible, avoid running errands before mealtime or nap time so your child is less likely to be cranky. If you're planning a longer trip, however, you may want to drive during nap time and let your child sleep in the car.

✋ If you know your child gets uncomfortable in the car, provide fresh air or a view of the road, or play his favorite songs or movies to make the car ride something he's eager to do.

Self-Talk

Don't tell yourself,

"On top of everything else I have to put up with, now my child is being stubborn."

Looking at your life as a series of problems will make you feel victimized, overwhelmed, and stressed-out. It will also set you up for self-pity and depression. Problems are always made worse by exaggeration and negative labels.

Instead, tell yourself,

"My child's stubbornness doesn't mean he'll always behave like this."

Adopting an optimistic attitude transforms your child's obstinacy into a temporary inconvenience, which frees your mind to patiently and proactively solve the problem.

Don't tell yourself,

"It's not worth the battle. I'll just forget about running my errands."
Giving up your agenda because of your child's resistance teaches him that whining is his ticket to getting his way. It also teaches him that giving up in the face of adversity is okay.

Instead, tell yourself,

"I don't need to give up what I want to do just because my child doesn't want to get in the car. I'll find a way to help him cooperate."
Having a positive attitude will model patience and perseverance and will help you solve the problem.

Don't tell yourself,

"My child thinks he can take advantage of me because I'm a single parent."
Blaming your child's resistance on the fact that you're a single parent establishes a victim mentality and sets up a win-or-lose approach to teaching him to cooperate—an unhealthy and unproductive mindset.

Instead, tell yourself,

"I understand how my child feels. I don't always want to do things I have to do."
Empathizing with your child helps elicit his desire to cooperate. When you support each other and work as a team, you can both reach your goals.

Talking to Your Child

Don't intimidate. Don't say,

"You get in the car right now or you'll be sorry!"
Threatening dire consequences tells your child that he can hold out until punishment is imminent; it doesn't teach him to cooperate. In addition, it forces you to follow through with punishment if he calls your bluff. If you don't follow through, you teach him that you don't always mean what you say. It's best to avoid both the threat and the need to follow through.

Instead, give choices. Say,

> **"You can choose to get in the car and have fun,
> or you can get in the car and be miserable. You decide."**

Helping him see the situation as his choice teaches him that he can decide how he wants to feel and helps him practice coping with things he doesn't like.

Don't bribe. Don't say,

> **"If you get in the car now, I'll give you a cookie."**

Bribing with treats gives food the unhealthy power to make your child happy. It also tells him that he can get a reward for his resistance.

Instead, make a deal. Say,

> **"When you're in your car seat and buckled up,
> then we can play your favorite songs and sing along.
> That's a happy thing to do in the car."**

Using Grandma's Rule teaches your child that he can have control and follow directions at the same time. When he cooperates, he gets to do enjoyable things.

Don't threaten. Don't say,

> **"If you don't get in the car right now, I'll have to spank you."**

The threat of corporal punishment teaches your child that violence is a consequence for not cooperating. Threatening violence also teaches him to cooperate only to avoid punishment, not because cooperation helps you accomplish mutually beneficial goals.

Instead, ask questions. Say,

> **"I understand that you don't want to get in the car,
> but I don't know why. Can you tell me?"**

Asking your child to tell you why he's refusing to cooperate gives him a chance to describe a problem you may not be aware of, such as not being able to see out the window or having an upset tummy. It also tells him that you care about his opinions and that you're glad he's willing to express them. When you discover the problem, you can address it instead of focusing on his disobedience.

Don't get angry. Don't say,
> *"I've asked you nicely three times. Now I'm getting mad!"*

Getting angry teaches him to follow directions only to avoid your anger, not to be a team player.

Instead, be positive. Say,
> *"I know you don't want to get in the car, but I need to get to work and you need to go to daycare. When you're in and buckled up, you can play with the special toys we keep in the car."*

Help your child understand that some requests are nonnegotiable, but the tasks can still be fun. Special toys and books in the car provide positive incentives for him to cooperate.

Chapter Three

"Please Sit in Your Car Seat."
"No! I Don't Wanna Sit in My Car Seat!"

Consider how you'd feel if you had to be strapped in a chair without understanding why. You'd have no interest in cooperating! So keep in mind how being "jailed" in the car seat must feel to your two-year-old, as you gently but firmly explain to her that it's very important for everyone to be buckled in safely. You're ultimately teaching her that some rules are nonnegotiable. Sitting in her car seat is one of them.

Helpful Hints

✋ Make rules about car travel, including staying safely buckled in until you reach your destination.

✋ Always wear your seat belt so your child will imitate your safety habits.

✋ Keep special toys and books in the car to keep your child entertained and to direct her attention away from her car seat.

Self-Talk

Don't tell yourself,
> *"I don't care if she's strapped in or not. I'm a safe driver."*
Making these kinds of excuses puts your child's safety in serious jeopardy. Her resistance shouldn't weaken your commitment to safety and good habits.

Instead, tell yourself,
> *"My goal is to make sure my child is safe,*
> *even if she doesn't understand the danger."*
Keeping your goals in mind will help you motivate your child to put safety first.

Don't tell yourself,

> *"Why is she so defiant? I must not get this parenting thing."*

Blaming yourself for your child's behavior won't help you solve the problem. You can't control her behavior—only she can. However, you can control your reaction to it.

Instead, tell yourself,

> *"I guess I wouldn't like to be strapped in my seat like that. It must make her feel powerless."*

Empathizing with your child's situation helps you relate to her feelings, which in turn helps her feel more inclined to cooperate.

Don't tell yourself,

> *"My mother told me I would have a defiant child."*

Blaming your child's uncooperative behavior on your parent's prediction is irrational and irrelevant. It not only takes away your responsibility for teaching your child appropriate behavior, it puts a label on her that could become a self-fulfilling prophecy.

Instead, tell yourself,

> *"My goal is to help my child learn to do things she doesn't want to do."*

By patiently helping your child understand why she needs to stay in her car seat, you're teaching her that cooperation will help keep her safe.

Talking to Your Child

Don't punish. Don't say,

> *"If you don't get in your car seat, I'll have to spank you."*

Threatening corporal punishment only teaches your child that you're bigger and stronger and can hurt her if she doesn't cooperate. Instead of threatening violence, inspire her cooperation by using empathy. Help her understand that you respect her feelings but that she nevertheless needs to do the safe thing.

Instead, ask questions. Say,

> *"What don't you like about sitting in your car seat?"*

Asking your child to tell you her reasons for refusing to sit in her car seat validates her feelings and teaches her to be empathetic. You may discover that she likes to see out the window but the car seat sits too low for her to do so, or that her car-seat buckle pinches her when you turn corners. You can correct these problems so she rides more comfortably.

Don't misuse authority. Don't say,
"If you don't stay in your car seat, a police officer will arrest you."
Don't use the police to threaten your child into cooperating. You want her to learn that police officers are her friends, not her enemies. Besides, a police officer is likely to arrest *you* if your child isn't buckled in.

Instead, remind her about the rule. Say,
"Sitting in your car seat is the rule.
The car can move only when you follow the car-seat rule."
Putting the rule in charge places you and your child on the same team, thereby reducing the chance that your child will fight with you and reinforcing the important lesson that rules govern our lives.

Don't get angry. Don't say,
"Now just get in your car seat!
You don't want me to get really mad, do you?"
Telling your child that she's responsible for your anger makes her feel guilty and erodes her ability to feel empathy. It may also give her an unwanted and unhealthy sense of power over your emotions.

Instead, use praise. Say,
"Thank you for getting in your car seat so nicely.
I appreciate your cooperation."
Praising your child's behavior teaches her that cooperation results in positive attention, something that motivates us all.

Don't bribe. Don't say,
"If you sit in your car seat, I'll give you a lollipop."
Bribing your child to follow the rules only teaches her that she should get a reward for doing what she's supposed to do.

Instead, make a deal. Say,
"When you sit in your car seat, we'll play the music you like."
This example of Grandma's Rule shows her that cooperation will generate positive consequences for everyone involved.

Chapter Four

"Please Get Out of the Car Now."
"No! I Don't Wanna Get Out of the Car!"

When your five-year-old refuses to leave the car, it may be time to review how many and what kinds of activities he's being shuttled to each day. If he's overloaded, his refusal to cooperate may be his way of telling you to stop his merry-go-round. It may also mean that he fears a particular activity or destination. Or he may simply want to stay home with you. Your first job, therefore, is to ask your child what he's thinking. His response will help you solve the problem.

Helpful Hints

🖐 Be open-minded, encouraging, and empathetic so your child will feel comfortable telling you his fears.

🖐 Establish rules about car behavior so your child understands what to expect when you reach a destination.

🖐 Practice your car routine before leaving home so the behaviors become automatic.

Self-Talk

Don't tell yourself,
> *"He never listens to me because he's such a defiant child.*
> *I don't know what I'm going to do with him."*

Labeling your child as defiant distracts you from the goal (teaching him to cooperate) by creating a problem (labeling, and thereby creating a self-fulfilling prophecy). If you convince yourself that your child is defiant, your goal of teaching him to cooperate will seem impossible to reach.

Instead, tell yourself,
> *"I know my child can choose to cooperate,*
> *and eventually he'll make this decision more often."*

Your opinion of what your child can do will help him believe he can do it, too. Be your child's best advocate.

Don't tell yourself,

"I give up. If he doesn't want to get out of the car, I'll just leave him there."

Telling yourself that the situation is hopeless may persuade you to do something dangerous and irrational, such as leaving your child alone in the car. Never make this choice!

Instead, tell yourself,

**"He can be stubborn sometimes,
but I need to keep his safety in mind at all times."**

Telling yourself that you can handle frustration increases your chances of doing so. Modeling responsible behavior and self-control is an important step in getting your child to learn these skills.

Don't tell yourself,

"I hate starting the day with a fight about getting out of the car."

Negative emotions damage a person's physical and emotional health. Research has shown that negative emotions cut off blood flow to the heart and decrease resistance to disease.[3]

Instead, tell yourself,

**"My child's refusal to get out of the car
doesn't mean the whole day is shot."**

Understanding that single events don't have to color the whole day keeps your outlook positive and lets you solve the problem. A positive outlook has been shown to help people think clearly and optimistically.[4]

Talking to Your Child

Don't beg. Don't say,

**"Won't you please get out of the car?
Mommy's tired and doesn't want to have to wait."**

Begging your child doesn't teach him how to cooperate. In fact, it may encourage him *not* to follow your directions so he can exercise his power and control.

Instead, give choices. Say,

**"Do you want to get of the car by yourself
or do you want me to help you out? You decide."**

Giving your child choices lets him practice making decisions and gives him a sense of power and control, two important motivators.

Don't bribe. Don't say,

"If you get out of the car now, I'll buy you a treat while we're in the store."

Bribing your child only teaches him that his cooperation can be bought.

Instead, make a deal. Say,

"When you get out of the car, we can get our shopping done and get back home so you can play."

Showing your child the long-term benefits of his decision can motivate him to endure the short-term frustration. In addition, this strategy teaches your child to respect the win-win method of decision making.

Don't use putdowns. Don't say,

"What's the matter with you? Why don't you ever do what you're told?"

Telling your child that he has a character flaw because he wants to exercise control over his life can lead him to view himself and his world pessimistically.

Instead, use incentives. Say,

"You're such a good helper when we're in the store. Let's get out of the car so you can help me shop."

Giving your child immediate incentives to do what you've asked can motivate him to cooperate. Telling him that you value his help increases his desire to follow your lead.

Don't threaten. Don't say,

"If you don't move now, mister, I'll give you something to be sorry about."

Threatening your child only encourages him to make threats to get what he wants; it doesn't show him peaceful ways to reach his goals.

Instead, invite feedback. Say,

"Help me understand why you don't want to get out of the car. If there's a problem, I'd like to help fix it."

Asking your child for feedback tells him that the situation isn't a crisis and that you care about his feelings—two good reasons for him to trust you. He may fear strangers or riding in the grocery cart, or he may worry about walking on the parking lot's hot asphalt.

Chapter Five

"Let's Get in the Elevator (or on the Escalator)." "No! I Don't Wanna Get in the Elevator!"

Walking into a closed box that moves up and down with a push of a button can be a scary experience for a three-year-old (as can stepping onto an escalator). It may make *you* a little nervous sometimes! Your child needs your patience and reassurance to help her adjust to these common forms of transportation.

Helpful Hints

✋ Familiarize your child with elevators and escalators by visiting them with her before you need to use them. Have her watch them from a distance so she can see that people get on and off safely. Explain how they work, if you think that will help ease her fear.

✋ Make sure there are alternatives to riding the elevator or escalator so you never find yourselves trapped in a situation in which you must use one or the other. Make sure you know where the stairs are, or park on the same level as the store you're planning to visit until your child is more comfortable riding the elevator or escalator.

Self-Talk

Don't tell yourself,
"People will think I'm an idiot because my child makes such a fuss in the elevator."
Believing that your child's behavior makes you look like a bad parent will only increase your anxiety and impatience with her.

Instead, tell yourself,
"Her meltdown at the elevator is no big deal."
Keeping parent-child conflicts in perspective and not taking them personally are the first steps in resolving them calmly and creatively. Once you consider these conflicts normal and inevitable, you can better understand and empathize with your child.

Don't tell yourself,

> *"I can't stand seeing her upset.*
> *We'll never use an elevator again because she hates it."*

Rescuing your child from her fears won't teach her how to cope with them.

Instead, tell yourself,

> *"It's okay for her to fear some things.*
> *I did when I was a child, and I survived."*

Accepting her behavior as developmentally normal will help both of you cope with the fears and will help you weather her storms with empathy.

Don't tell yourself,

> *"What did I do wrong to have such a fearful child?"*

Blaming yourself for your child's feelings sets you up for a lifetime of guilt. You don't control your child's feelings; she does.

Instead, tell yourself,

> *"Her fears aren't my fault."*

Understanding that she owns her feelings helps you separate yourself from her fears and validates your ability to help her overcome them.

Talking to Your Child

Don't isolate her. Don't say,

> *"Come on, toughen up. You need to face your fears."*

The "toughen up" approach tells your child that she must deal with her fears alone. It doesn't show her how to overcome them.

Instead, offer solutions. Say,

> *"I understand that you don't want to ride the elevator.*
> *We can take the stairs and maybe try the elevator next time."*

Showing empathy for your child's feelings will help her feel safe in your presence, which will help bolster her confidence for future excursions. Suggesting possible solutions gives her proactive ways of handling the fear.

Don't use putdowns. Don't say,

> *"Don't be such a crybaby!"*

Labeling your child a crybaby creates a negative self-image, tells her she's flawed, and can become a self-fulfilling prophecy.

Instead, be positive. Say,

> *"I know the elevator was scary before, but you're much braver and stronger now. I think you can handle it, if you want."*

Validating your child's strength will help her feel your support and will encourage her to overcome her fears.

Don't threaten. Don't say,

> *"If you cry again at the elevator, I'll give you a spanking. Then you'll really have something to cry about."*

Threats only create more fears and show your child that you're willing to hurt her rather than help her when she doesn't want to do what you ask.

Instead, make it fun. Say,

> *"I'll hold you in my arms while we're in the elevator, so you'll feel safe. I like the feeling in my tummy when the elevator goes up and down. It's kind of exciting!"*

Helping your child label her fear as excitement lets her accept and even enjoy the feelings she feared before, as she reframes her experience.

Don't bribe. Don't say,

> *"Baby, if you'll just go on the escalator and be quiet, I'll give you some candy."*

Bribing your child to gain her cooperation won't help her overcome her fears. It will only teach her that not cooperating gets rewarded.

Instead, show her other options. Say,

> *"Using the stairs will be good exercise for us until you feel okay about using the escalator. Maybe next time we can try the escalator and see how fast we can get to the top."*

Showing your child other options prevents her from feeling trapped. Doing so also teaches her to weigh the costs and benefits of each option, which is good practice in decision making.

Chapter Six

"It's Time to Get on the Airplane."
"No! I Don't Wanna Get on the Airplane!"

Whether you're an experienced flier or a nervous first-timer, air travel creates more anxiety than ever before. Your five-year-old may have heard you talk about safety concerns surrounding air travel, or he may have seen reports on television about plane crashes or hijackings. To address your child's fear of getting on a plane, emphasize the benefits of air travel and reassure him that his safety is your number one concern.

Helpful Hints

🖐 Before booking your flight, think about your child's ability to tolerate schedule changes, deal with the hustle and bustle of the airport, sit for several hours buckled in a seat, and handle his fear of flying.

🖐 Consider other travel options, if necessary, taking into account the time it will take to reach your destination and the costs and benefits of each mode of transportation. Also consider your child's need for frequent potty stops and other special concerns.

🖐 Put yourself in your child's shoes by thinking about what it might be like to be a little person who's had no experience with big events, such as flying in an airplane.

🖐 Watch what you say. Even casual comments about being afraid to fly can be contagious. Calm yourself by keeping in mind that the chance of dying in a plane crash is one in nine million.[5]

Self-Talk

Don't tell yourself,
"My relatives will hate me if we don't go."
Fearing what others might think of you focuses your attention on something you can't control and increases your anxiety over your child's lack of cooperation. Both decrease your chances of getting your child on the airplane calmly.

Instead, tell yourself,

> *"I need to stay focused on helping my child cope with getting*
> *on the airplane, not on what my relatives might think."*

Shifting your focus from your relatives to your child will prevent the problem from becoming overwhelming and will avoid needless distress.

Don't tell yourself,

> *"My kid's not normal because he doesn't want to fly in an airplane."*

Telling yourself what your child should or shouldn't fear isn't rational. How he feels or what he fears isn't something you can control. You can control only *your* feelings, not anyone else's.

Instead, tell yourself,

> *"My child's fear of flying helps me learn something about him."*

It's common for people of all ages to fear the unknown, especially events over which they have little or no control. Although your child may be a cautious preschooler now, he can learn to view his world as an adventure, not a danger.

Don't tell yourself,

> *"My poor child has my stupid fear of flying!"*

Blaming yourself for your child's fears won't help either of you overcome them.

Instead, tell yourself,

> *"Coping with my own fear of flying will help me guide him through his."*

Knowing your strengths and weaknesses will help you empathize with your child's feelings.

Don't tell yourself,

> *"He'll never be able to ride in an airplane if we don't take this trip."*

It's irrational to demand that your child cooperate out of concern that he'll never be able to overcome his fear otherwise.

Instead, tell yourself,

> *"My goal is to help my child understand*
> *and cope with his fear of flying."*

Understanding your role as a teaching parent will help you and your child learn from every challenge. In this case, you need to work on helping him prepare for future airplane rides.

Talking to Your Child

Don't use putdowns. Don't say,

> *"What's wrong with you? I thought you'd love to fly in an airplane. You're such a difficult child."*

These words tell your child that there must be something wrong with him because he expressed his feelings. This will lead him to view himself and his world pessimistically. In addition, you'll discourage him from telling you when he feels upset.

Instead, role-play. Say,

> *"Let's pretend we're going on a plane trip. You be the passenger, and I'll be the flight attendant, the person who brings snacks and drinks and helps us stay safe while we're flying."*

By role-playing what happens on a plane, you can teach your child what to expect and thereby ease his fear of flying.

Don't issue an ultimatum. Don't say,

> *"Listen to me, mister! We're going on the plane and there are no two ways about it!"*

Drawing a line in the sand polarizes the situation and forces your child to dig in more deeply to protect his position.

Instead, invite feedback. Say,

> *"Tell me how your tummy feels when you think about getting on that big airplane."*

If he describes "butterflies" or another feeling he gets when he's scared, then anxiety is driving his resistance. Help him understand and label his feelings, which is the first step toward helping him recognize and overcome his fears.

Don't use guilt. Don't say,

> *"Wait until your grandmother hears that you didn't want to come visit her. She'll be really mad at you, and you'll be sorry."*

Threatening your child with the loss of his grandparent's approval won't teach him to cope with his fears; it will only increase his sense of shame and reduce his ability to empathize with his grandparent.

Instead, be positive. Say,

> *"Flying on a plane to visit Grandma in her new house will be a great adventure! We'll have fun playing on the beach and discovering what's in Grandma's secret drawers."*

Talking about all the fun you'll have may help your child manage his fears, and he may begin to see flying as simply a means to an end.

Don't label. Don't say,

> *"That's okay, honey. Mom's a worrier, too."*

This tells your child that he won't be able to stop worrying because it's a part of him, just as it's a part of you.

Instead, use empathy. Say,

> *"I understand that it's scary to go on an airplane.*
> *Sometimes I feel a little scared, too.*
> *But I just tell myself that I'm brave and strong and can do it."*

Telling your child about your fears and the self-talk you use to overcome them teaches him an important skill and makes it easier for him to tell you how he feels. In addition, it helps him understand that his feelings are normal and manageable.

Don't bribe. Don't say,

> *"If you go on the airplane with us,*
> *we'll buy you that new bike you've been wanting."*

Bribing children to get them to do what you want only leads them to expect a tangible reward for cooperating. Your goal is to encourage your child's internal motivation to cooperate, not to provide external rewards for doing what you ask.

Instead, validate his importance. Say,

> *"You're a terrific helper with the baby.*
> *Can you help me keep track of the diaper bag*
> *to make sure it gets on the plane with us?"*

Making your child your helper gives him something positive to think about and increases his sense of control. It also gives him a way to be a team player. He'll want to cooperate because he's needed.

Chapter Seven

"Let's Hold Hands in the Store."
"No! I Don't Wanna Hold Hands!"

Mobile two-year-olds find malls and grocery stores filled with enchanting possibilities, and they see a parent's hand as the enemy of freedom. It's only natural for your child to want to run free; there's just so much to see and do. To avoid quashing her curiosity, creatively enforce the rules about staying close.

Helpful Hints

꙳ Avoid shopping during (or shortly before) mealtime or nap time.

꙳ Keep young children in a stroller so you can focus on teaching older children to stay close.

Self-Talk

Don't tell yourself,
> *"I don't know what to do when my child refuses to hold my hand. I'm never sure I'm doing the right thing."*

Expecting a "right" solution to every parenting problem is unrealistic. A solution fits when it matches your (and your child's) perspective, personality, and comfort level.

Instead, tell yourself,
> *"I can handle this. My goal is to teach my child to hold my hand when we're in the store."*

Appreciate your child's curiosity about her world, but don't compromise her safety. If she continues to resist your request to hold hands, you may need to shop without her for a time.

Don't tell yourself,

> *"I'm scared that she'll get lost, but I don't want her to be mad at me."*

You need to be your child's leader, not her friend. She won't always like what you say and do, and you won't always like what she says and does. Focus on keeping her safe rather than pleasing her.

Instead, tell yourself,

> *"Safety rules are important and need to be followed."*

Affirming your views on safety will help you stand firm when she tests the rule.

Don't tell yourself,

> *"I have to show her I'm mad or she won't know how important holding my hand is."*

Using anger to motivate your child's cooperation will diminish her ability to feel empathy and will model negative behavior.

Instead, tell yourself,

> *"Getting mad at her will only make the situation worse."*

Choosing to get angry will prevent you from thinking through the problem and finding ways to solve it.

Talking to Your Child

Don't threaten. Don't say,

> *"You get back here and hold my hand or you'll get a spanking!"*

Threatening physical punishment only increases your child's desire to stay away from you. She may ultimately comply with your demand out of fear and to avoid getting hurt, but she won't do so because it's the safe thing to do.

Instead, remind her about the rule. Say,

> *"Remember, the rule is that we're supposed to hold hands from the time we leave the car to the time we get back. We have to follow the rule in order to stay safe."*

Reminding your child of the rule makes the rule the "bad guy" rather than you. It also focuses your child's attention on the tasks to be learned: staying safe and following directions.

Don't bribe. Don't say,
"If you hold my hand while we're shopping, I'll buy you a new toy."
Don't give gifts for doing what you ask. You want your child to hold your hand so she'll be safe, not so she'll get a gift. Bribery distracts your child's attention from the goals: learning to be safe and learning to cooperate.

Instead, practice. Before you leave home, say,
"We're going shopping this afternoon, so let's practice how you're going to hold my hand. Then we can keep each other safe."
Practicing the rule transforms it into a conditioned set of behaviors; your child learns to automatically do what you expect.

Don't punish. Don't say,
*"If you don't hold my hand,
I won't let you watch TV when we get home."*
Threatening to take away privileges won't teach your child to cooperate; it will, however, teach her to make threats to get someone to do what she wants.

Instead, use empathy. Say,
"I know it's hard to hang on to my hand when you see so many things you like, but staying close is the rule. It's important and it keeps us safe."
Model empathy for your child by telling her that you understand her desire to explore her world, but remind her that she still needs to follow the rule.

Don't label. Don't say,
"What's the matter with you? Don't you know it's dangerous to run away from me? That was a stupid thing to do!"
Labels and putdowns tell your child that there's something wrong with her because she wants to follow her natural curiosity. This isn't the way to encourage cooperation.

Instead, find other options. Say,
"It seems that holding my hand isn't comfortable for you. How about hanging on to my skirt (or belt, or purse, or pant leg)? That way I'll know where you are and neither of us will get lost."
Finding alternative handholds for your child can also free your hands for other tasks. It's a win-win solution.

Don't boss. Don't say,

> *"Don't wander off, and don't touch anything!"*

These admonitions only tell your child what she's *not* supposed to do; they don't remind her of what she's supposed to do or why she's supposed to do it. They're also impractical for a young child who's eager to explore.

Instead, use praise. Say,

> *"Thank you for holding my hand.*
> *I feel so good knowing that we're together and safe."*

Praising cooperative behavior encourages your child to keep up the good work and tells her that following the rule gets positive attention from you.

Chapter Eight

"It's Time to Go to Daycare."
"No! I Don't Wanna Go to Daycare!"

Your guilt meter can skyrocket when you announce that it's time to go to daycare and your three-year-old cries, "I want to stay home with *you!*" First, investigate the daycare situation to make sure there are no individuals, situations, or procedures that are making him fearful. When you're confident there's no problem, then you can focus on his difficulty with separation, a common problem for young children.

Helpful Hints

🖐 Before your child begins regular daycare, give him some practice being away from you, and teach him that you'll always return. Take him to your daycare provider or leave him with a qualified babysitter for an hour or two a few times a week to get him used to the idea.

🖐 Avoid complaining about your job and how much you hate putting your child in daycare. Your negativity is contagious.

🖐 Keep goodbyes short and sweet to help your child make the transition to his new environment quickly and smoothly.

Self-Talk

Don't tell yourself,
> *"I should be with my child. I wish I didn't have to go to work, so he could be home with me."*

Feeling guilty about needing (or wanting) to work suggests that you've done something wrong by putting him in daycare. Remind yourself that you're doing what's best for you and your child. Daycare gives him the opportunity to be with other children, and working enables you to provide for your family.

Instead, tell yourself,
> **"I'm doing what's best for my family."**

Make sure that the daycare environment is safe and nurturing and that the providers are loving, responsible people who share your parenting philosophy.

Don't tell yourself,
> **"My child puts me in such a bad mood when he fights going to daycare."**

Feeling sorry for yourself is counterproductive and may lead to guilt and depression. *You* control how you feel, not your child.

Instead, tell yourself,
> **"Resisting daycare is my child's way of telling me that he has problems with separation right now."**

Struggling with separation is normal for young children. It's your job to help him practice separating from you and to teach him to work and play with others.

Don't tell yourself,
> **"If only my ex hadn't left me, I wouldn't have to go to work and my child could stay home with me."**

Blaming your ex-spouse for your having to work will only increase the tension between you and will possibly alienate your child from his other parent.

Instead, tell yourself,
> **"Just because my child has to go to daycare doesn't make me or my ex a bad parent."**

Avoiding the blame game will keep you, your child, and your child's other parent on course as you work together to provide what's best for everyone involved.

Talking to Your Child

Don't threaten. Don't say,
> **"Stop screaming and hold still while I get you dressed, or I'll give you something to scream about!"**

Threatening your child only encourages him to resist further in order to test whether you'll follow through with your threat. It also teaches him that bigger, stronger people can use violence to get their way.

Instead, praise cooperative behavior. Say,

"Thanks for letting me put your socks on.
That was really helpful. We'll be ready for daycare in no time!"

It may be difficult to praise your child when he's challenging you at every turn, but do your best to encourage *any* sign of cooperation. For example, say, "You're eating your breakfast so nicely! That means you're going to have lots of energy today!" or, "Thanks for telling me about the things you like at daycare. When you talk about things you like, I know you feel good!"

Don't name-call. Don't say,

"You're such a brat! Now shut up and get in your car seat!"

Intimidating your child by calling him names is counterproductive. Name-calling may also become a self-fulfilling prophecy as your child learns to live up to his label.

Instead, offer support. Say,

"I'll talk to Miss Sara at daycare to make sure everything's okay."

It's always wise to find out as much as possible about what's going on at daycare when your child is reluctant to go. Ask your daycare provider how your child behaves after you leave, who he plays with, what new things might be going on, and what suggestions she might have to ease your child's discomfort.

Don't label. Don't say,

"Sweetheart, I know you're really shy and don't like
to be around other kids, but Mommy needs to go to work."

Labeling your child as shy may make the label a permanent part of his identity. It tells him that he can't play with other children because that's not who he is.

Instead, provide emotional support. Say,

"Would you like to take your teddy bear to daycare today?
He always makes you feel good when you hold him close."

Sometimes children like to take a "lovie" with them when they're feeling reluctant to go somewhere. A lovie can soothe a child when parents aren't around to do so.

Don't bribe. Don't say,

> *"If you'll stop screaming and get in the car, I'll buy you a jelly donut on the way to daycare. You know how you like jelly donuts."*

Bribing children only teaches them to expect a reward every time they make a fuss. In addition, using food as a reward will cause your child to associate food with love and nurturing, which may lead to eating disorders.

Instead, use Grandma's Rule. Say,

> *"When you go to daycare without a fuss, then we'll go to the park when I pick you up this afternoon."*

Grandma's Rule teaches your child that he can have fun doing what he wants after he's cooperated with your request.

Don't use guilt and blame. Don't say,

> *"You know I have to work to buy you clothes and toys! Don't make me late again!"*

Using guilt and blame won't motivate your child to cooperate with you or teach him how to cope with separation. Instead, it will tell him that *he's* responsible for your choices, such as going to work.

Instead, shift the focus. Say,

> *"I'll go to my job, you'll go to yours, and we'll both be home for dinner tonight!"*

Framing your child's separation as temporary and focusing his attention on being with you later can help him cope with going to daycare.

Don't give in. Don't say,

> *"Well, if you don't want to go to daycare, then I'll stay home with you."*

You may be tempted to give up your obligations in order to stay home with your child, but giving in only teaches him that his resistance will get him what he wants.

Instead, teach him to delay gratification. Say,

> *"Today is a workday for me and a daycare day for you. Let's count the days till we both have a stay-at-home day!"*

Helping your child focus on a desirable future event will teach him the important skill of delaying gratification. Embracing this teachable moment to help your child practice separating from you is the productive and healthy response.

Chapter Nine

"Let's Go to Your Lesson."
"No! I Don't Wanna Go to My Lesson!"

When you read about Tiger Woods's prowess with a golf club at age five, you may be disappointed when your preschooler balks at going to golf lessons. A good first step toward gaining your child's cooperation is considering her personality, her schedule, and whether her resistance is ongoing or occasional. Is she reluctant to try new things? Is she unable to sit and focus for several minutes? Does she lack the ability to follow through? Does she have unscheduled free time? Does she say she hates her teacher? Is this the first time she's resisted going? Understanding your child and the circumstances surrounding her resistance will give you insight into why she's protesting this learning opportunity.

Helpful Hints

🖐 Interview the teachers before enrolling your child in an activity. Find out if their educational and disciplinary philosophies are a good match for you and your child. The most effective teachers are ones who empathize with children, communicate well with them, and treat them with respect.

🖐 Make sure your child understands the rules about listening to instructions, following directions, practicing, and sticking to the routine.

🖐 Make sure your child has the ability to do (or learn) all the things that will be required of her during the activity.

Self-Talk

Don't tell yourself,

"Children should obey their parents because parents know best."
This authoritarian approach will set you up for never-ending power struggles with your headstrong preschooler. Realizing that you can't control your child's behavior—only your *reaction* to it—is the first step toward guiding that behavior toward the desired goal.

Instead, tell yourself,

"I can put up with a little resistance. It's not that big a deal."
By framing your reaction in positive, coping terms, you send your child the message that you support her voicing her opinions even if they differ from yours. Keep in mind that the long-term goal of parenting is to raise independent, self-sufficient, well-adjusted human beings.

Don't tell yourself,

"Every child should take music lessons to get ahead in life."
Avoid buying into myths that tell you that there's one path to success.

Instead, tell yourself,

"It's not really important for her to take lessons now. She can wait awhile."
A look at your child's schedule may lead you to conclude that she's too busy to continue this activity. Just because your child is reluctant to go now doesn't mean she won't clamor for lessons later.

Don't tell yourself,

"Something must be wrong with my child. Everyone thinks gymnastics lessons are fun. I did."
Projecting your likes and dislikes onto your child won't help you understand her resistance. In fact, it may make you push her into activities for *your* sake, not hers.

Instead, tell yourself,

"Just because I liked gymnastics doesn't mean my child should."
Consider who originally wanted the lessons—you or your child. Ideally, both of you did. Keep in mind that your child may not be well suited for something you'd like her to do, and that she may change her mind once she's started.

Talking to Your Child

Don't threaten. Don't say,

"I'm sick and tired of your attitude. You'll do what I say or get a spanking!"
Telling your child that you'll hurt her if she resists teaches her two undesirable lessons: using violence is an acceptable way to solve problems, and it's okay to hurt someone when you're angry.

Instead, ask questions. Say,

> **"What don't you like about your lessons?**
> **Is there anything I can do to help make them more fun?"**

When you calmly ask such questions, you gain a greater understanding of your child's concerns and tell her that you care about her thoughts and feelings.

Don't use guilt. Don't say,

> **"What's the matter with you?**
> **You begged me to let you take these lessons!"**

Asking what's wrong with her implies that there *is* something wrong with her because she changed her mind.

Instead, reframe the situation. Say,

> **"Let's think about all the fun you'll have when you go to your lesson."**

Changing your child's perspective can help her overcome her reluctance to participate. Motivate her by helping her see how rewarding and fun the experience can be.

Don't bribe. Don't say,

> **"If you get dressed right now and get in the car before**
> **I count to ten, I'll buy you a treat on the way home."**

Promising your child an external reward for doing what you've asked teaches her to do something only to get a reward. Your objective is to teach her that it feels good to do something for its own sake.

Instead, show her how to appreciate her progress. Say,

> **"Let's make a star chart that we can put on the**
> **refrigerator to show how many lessons you've completed."**

Encouraging your child to track her progress is an excellent way to promote self-motivation and cooperation.

Don't shame and blame. Don't say,

> **"I'm so disappointed in you. You never finish what you start."**

Shaming your child teaches her that your love is conditional—that you love her only when she does what you ask.

Instead, offer choices. Say,

> **"Let's try five more lessons.**
> **After that you can see whether you still like them or not."**

Decide on a goal with a definite endpoint in mind so your child won't feel trapped and helpless. This approach also gives her a sense of control over the decision making.

Chapter Ten

"Let's Go to Practice."
"No! I Don't Wanna Go to Practice!"

Some toddlers and preschoolers may love the routine of practicing a sport, but others may balk at it. If your child is putting up consistent resistance, the sport or coach may not be a good fit. If his resistance is occasional, he may be struggling with issues such as ability, teamwork, and sportsmanship.

Helpful Hints

W Before enrolling your child in a sport, decide whether he has both the interest and the physical ability for it. Practice at home to evaluate these important prerequisites.

W Think about whether your child can understand instructions, pay attention, and sustain the physical effort required by a sport.

W Make sure the adults in the program share your educational and disciplinary philosophies, and that they communicate kindly and effectively with children.

W Think about your rules for your child's involvement in a sport, including how long he may stay involved, what options he has for withdrawing, and how much support he can expect from you.

Self-Talk

Don't tell yourself,

"He knows I've always wanted him to be a great soccer player. I can't believe he's disappointing me like this."

This is not about you. Being disappointed in your child because he doesn't fulfill your dreams is unhealthy for both of you. Take his reluctance to practice as an indication that he's tired or that something is happening at practice that he doesn't like.

Instead, tell yourself,

"I know that soccer is my dream, not his."

Separating your desires from your child's will help you focus on understanding *his* reasons for not wanting to practice.

Don't tell yourself,

"What will the other parents think if my kid doesn't show up at practice?"

Worrying about what others think prevents you from focusing on your child. Don't waste energy on things you can't control.

Instead, tell yourself,

"It's important to teach my child the relationship between practice and mastery."

Help your child understand that one needs to practice in order to learn to do something well.

Don't tell yourself,

"He'll never be popular if he doesn't play well. So he needs to practice."

Life isn't a popularity contest. Your child will establish friendships whether he plays a sport well or not. Using words like *never* creates a helpless, hopeless attitude that's unhealthy and unproductive.

Instead, tell yourself,

"I need to help my child understand that hard work will increase his chance of succeeding."

Focusing on the long-term goal of playing a sport well (if that's what he wants) can help your child understand the importance of practicing. Encourage his cooperation so he can realize his goal, not so he can impress others.

Don't tell yourself,

"I can't stand fat, lazy kids, and he's going to become one if he doesn't practice."

Jumping to dire conclusions about your child's fate is irrational and puts unnecessary pressure on him. It won't teach him to follow through with his responsibilities. In addition, focusing your attention on his weight and appearance may increase his risk of developing self-image problems.

Instead, tell yourself,

"My goal is to help my child develop healthy habits."

Habits that are modeled and reinforced during the preschool years are likely to become lifelong behaviors.

Talking to Your Child

Don't shame. Don't say,

"I'm disappointed with you. You're going to grow up to be a lazy bum."

Shaming your child will only make him think badly of himself. If it does motivate him, it will only be to please you rather than to follow his dream of playing the sport he loves.

Instead, invite feedback. Say,

"Tell me what you don't like about going to practice."

If you learn that he dislikes how he's treated, you can take appropriate steps to remedy the situation. If it's because he doesn't like the tedium and repetition, teach him ways to overcome his boredom. Help him stay in love with the sport even when he dislikes the rigors of practice.

Don't threaten. Don't say,

"If you don't get ready for soccer practice right now, mister, you won't be watching any TV for the rest of the week."

These kinds of threats won't motivate your child to love soccer or to cooperate with you in the future. They will only lead to more battles when he wants to watch TV.

Instead, use empathy. Say,

"I know you don't want to go to practice, but sometimes we have to do hard stuff so we can enjoy other things later."

Help your child understand that practice may not make him perfect, but it will help him feel more comfortable with the bat, ball, or other sports equipment. Work with the coach to motivate your child to learn that following through is important in reaching his goals.

Don't bribe. Don't say,

> *"If you go to T-ball practice today,*
> *I'll buy you that new action figure you want."*

Bribing your child to do what you want only teaches him to expect some external reward every time you make a request. Instead, encourage him to do something for the personal satisfaction and happiness it brings. This will teach him the value of cooperation much more effectively.

Instead, make a deal. Say,

> *"When you go to T-ball practice and work hard, then we can*
> *work on your tree house together like you've been wanting."*

Using Grandma's Rule tells your child that he has to do what's necessary before doing what he wants. In addition, it teaches him to understand that his agenda and yours are both important.

Don't label. Don't say,

> *"Well, I guess you're just a klutz like your cousin, Philip.*
> *He can't walk without falling down."*

Labeling your child as inept will only make him feel worse about himself and his abilities.

Instead, be helpful. Say,

> *"Let's make a practice chart."*

Making a chart that shows how your child's skills are improving can help motivate him to continue practicing. For example, record the number of times he kicked the ball into the goal at soccer practice or hit the ball at T-ball practice.

Chapter Eleven

"It's Time to Go to Daddy's (or Mommy's) House."
"No! I Don't Wanna Go to Daddy's House!"

Learning to shuttle between different homes can be difficult for you and your four-year-old. The adjustment takes time and effort, so patience is the key. How you respond to your child's protests will depend on your level of empathy and your attitude toward the situation. Arrange to have a set of your child's favorite comfort items at both locations, or ensure that you and your child's other parent transport the comfort items with each move, so your child feels at home in both places.

Helpful Hints

👋 Post a schedule to show your child when she's supposed to go to her other parent's home, or give her periodic verbal reminders.

👋 Work hard to communicate a positive attitude about your child's other parent.

👋 Promote your child's healthy development by making sure you and your child's other parent agree upon discipline methods that are respectful and that reinforce your mutual love for your child.

Self-Talk

Don't tell yourself,
"Isn't it great that my child likes my home better?"
Celebrating your child's preference for your home creates a destructive, competitive relationship with your child's other parent. As long as he or she provides a safe environment, keep a positive attitude about your child spending time there, regardless of your feelings about the other parent.

Instead, tell yourself,

> *"Although I'm more comfortable when my child is with me,*
> *I know it's important for her to spend time with her dad (or mom)."*

Empathizing with your child's needs lets you do what's best for her. In addition, being supportive of her other parent will encourage her to feel comfortable staying with that parent.

Don't tell yourself,

> *"I need to make my house more fun than my ex's place,*
> *so my child will want to stay here."*

Competing with your child's other parent for "favorite parent" status can become a never-ending battle. Your job is to help your child realize that both her parents love her unconditionally.

Instead, tell yourself,

> *"Just because my child is putting up a fuss*
> *doesn't mean she doesn't like her other home."*

Avoid interpreting your child's protest as a rejection of her other home. Support her going there, if you know it's a healthy, supportive environment.

Talking to Your Child

Don't belittle. Don't say,

> *"I don't care what you want. You're going to your father's*
> *(or mother's) house. So shut up and get in the car."*

Your lack of empathy will only increase your child's desire to be with you in order to regain your love that she fears she might be losing.

Instead, use empathy. Say,

> *"I understand that you want to stay here,*
> *but the rules tell us that tonight you go to your father's*
> *(or mother's) house. You can call me before you go to sleep."*

Using the rule to govern the situation helps avoid conflict between you and your child. Suggesting that she call you helps her know that your love and support are always nearby.

Don't disparage your child's other parent. Don't say,

> *"Your father (or mother) is always trying*
> *to avoid spending time with you."*

Suggesting that the other parent doesn't want to be with your child will damage her ability to feel comfortable moving between homes. Your words are powerful tools for promoting love or hate, so choose them carefully.

Instead, reinforce a loving environment. Say,

> *"Yes, you can stay here on Wednesday. But today is Monday,*
> *your day to go to your daddy's (or mommy's).*
> *He (or she) is looking forward to spending time with you."*

Remind your child of the good things that happen in her other parent's care. This creates a win-win situation in which everyone's needs are met. It also keeps conflict at bay.

Don't give in. Don't say,

> *"Okay, go ahead and stay here. I don't care what you do."*

Although it may seem as if you're doing your child a favor by letting her stay, telling her that you don't care what she does suggests that you don't care about her. It also says that you'll give in when she puts up a little resistance.

Instead, ask for feedback. Say,

> *"I know you want to stay here today, but you'll have lots of fun at*
> *your daddy's house. What kinds of things do you do there?"*

Asking your child for feedback may give you insight into why the other home isn't desirable and what you might do to improve the situation. It also tells your child that you support her going there.

Chapter Twelve

"It's Time to Go to Your Swimming Lesson." "No! I Don't Wanna Go to Swimming!"

Swimming lessons are more punishment than pleasure for children who have no interest in learning to swim, or for parents who fear the water. Try to keep your comments positive, even if swimming is not your thing. Promote the importance of knowing how to swim, and explain the rules that govern your child's behavior near water, especially if you live near a lake, river, or stream.

Helpful Hints

✋ When children are exposed to water play as infants, they're more likely to love learning to swim.

✋ Play games in the bathtub so your child learns to be comfortable in the water.

✋ Make sure the swimming instructor, pool location, and water temperature are well suited to your child's learning style.

✋ Avoid complaining about looking fat or skinny in a bathing suit, to avoid sending your child the message that being one or the other is undesirable.

Self-Talk

Don't tell yourself,
"It's so stupid for him to be afraid of the water."
Telling yourself that your child's fears are stupid relieves you of the responsibility of helping him overcome his fear.

Instead, tell yourself,
"My job is to help him overcome his fear of the water."
Understand that fear is a survival instinct. Your child will overcome his fear when he no longer believes that water is dangerous.

Don't tell yourself,

"I feel so guilty about passing my fear of water on to my child."

Blaming yourself for your child's fears assumes that you can make your child feel any way you want. It's more productive to focus on teaching him water safety skills.

Instead, tell yourself,

"I know he doesn't like the water now, but I'm confident that he'll learn to be more comfortable in it."

Telling yourself there will be a positive outcome promotes good mental and physical health.

Don't tell yourself,

"I'm so embarrassed that my child refuses to go to the pool with my friends and their kids."

Don't choose to be embarrassed because of your child's reluctance to cooperate. It's irrational to think that something's wrong with him because he isn't ready to learn to swim.

Instead, tell yourself,

"My goal is to help my child learn to be comfortable in the water."

Keeping your goal in mind will help you overcome any negative thoughts about your child's resistance. Focus on helping him reach the goal, not on his refusal to cooperate.

Don't tell yourself,

"I don't care if he ever learns to swim."

Giving up on your child compromises his safety and teaches him to stop trying when confronted by fear.

Instead, tell yourself,

"Learning to swim is important for my child's safety, so I'll keep helping him with lessons."

Stick to your agenda to teach your child to be safe around water and to show him that persistence pays off.

Talking to Your Child

Don't bully. Don't say,
> *"You're going to take swimming lessons whether you like it or not."*

Your lack of empathy and militant enforcement of lessons tells your child that you don't care enough about his feelings to motivate him through supportive teaching. Ask yourself how you'd feel if you didn't want to take swimming lessons but were forced to do so.

Instead, invite feedback. Say,
> *"Tell me what you don't like about swimming."*

Seeking your child's feedback will help you understand his reservations. Chances are he doesn't like to get his face wet or doesn't want to go underwater. Show him you're on his team by empathizing with his fears.

Don't give in. Don't say,
> *"That's okay, honey.*
> *You don't have to do anything you don't want to do."*

Don't give your child veto power over something that's important for his safety. Doing so will prevent him from gaining the skills he needs to persevere when something doesn't come easily.

Instead, use empathy. Say,
> *"I know you don't want to take lessons, but learning how*
> *to swim is important. And I know it's hard to do things you*
> *don't want to do, so I'll be right here by the side of the pool."*

Reaffirming the importance of swimming and reassuring your child that you'll be nearby will help reduce his anxiety. In addition, you'll be reminding him that he has a cheerleader when he needs a boost.

Don't bribe. Don't say,
> *"If you take lessons, then I'll let you have a puppy."*

Teaching your child the fine art of cooperation shouldn't include giving him a gift for doing what you ask. He'll think that doing something he doesn't want to do should always earn a reward.

Instead, make a deal. Say,

> **"When you cooperate with your swimming instructor,
> then you can come home and play with your friends."**

Grandma's Rule tells your child that he can do what he wants to do when he has done what he has to do. This promise of meeting his agenda after he meets yours teaches him to be flexible and to delay gratification.

Don't shame. Don't say,

> **"You're not going to embarrass me again by screaming
> and crying at the pool, are you? Don't be such a baby!"**

Calling your child names tells him that your love is conditional. You're teaching him to put others down when they don't live up to his expectations—a lesson you don't want him to learn.

Instead, be supportive. Say,

> **"I know you don't want to take swimming lessons,
> but you're brave and strong and can do it."**

Acknowledge your child's reluctance as well as his bravery. Assure him that you understand his fears while reminding him that he has the strength to overcome them. This will improve his self-confidence and allow him to face other difficulties in the future.

SECTION II
GETTING DRESSED

Our dilemma is that we hate change and
love it at the same time. What we really want is
for things to remain the same but get better.
—*Sidney J. Harris*

Chapter Thirteen

"Please Put On Clean Clothes."
"No! I Wanna Wear My Dirty Clothes!"

Favorite clothes are like old friends, no matter how young or old you are. Therefore, respect your four-year-old's desire to wear the same clothes day after day, but don't back down from the rule of wearing clean clothes. Let her know that a washing machine will only temporarily separate her from her beloved outfit. How happy she'll be when it "comes back home."

Helpful Hints

🖐 Establish a rule about wearing clean clothes, and make sure your child understands the definition of *dirty*. For example, "We wear clothes that don't smell bad and don't have stains."

🖐 Talk about the importance of cleanliness so your child understands why you need to wash clothes regularly.

🖐 Let your child help with the laundry so she can see how clothes go through the washer and dryer and come out clean.

Self-Talk

Don't tell yourself,
"I know I shouldn't give in, but I'm tired of fighting with her. I don't care what she wears."
Your lack of persistence teaches your child that you don't mean what you say and that it's okay to give up when confronted with a challenge.

Instead, tell yourself,
"I'm eager to teach her that wearing clean clothes feels good."
Reframing the problem as an opportunity to teach an important lesson keeps you excited and positive about the long-term goal of wearing clean clothes.

Don't tell yourself,

> ### *"She should know better than to want to wear dirty clothes. What's wrong with her?"*

Don't judge your child based on what she wants to wear. Such judgments teach her that her decisions sometimes make her less worthwhile, which may lead her to try to be perfect in order to gain your love. Everyone makes mistakes, and you need to see mistakes as ways to learn what you didn't know.

Instead, tell yourself,

> ### *"Wanting to wear the same dress all the time isn't such a big deal."*

Realize that preschool children often resist change, then go about the business of helping your child learn to cope with change.

Don't tell yourself,

> ### *"What will the teachers think if she goes to school in the same outfit every day?"*

When you catch yourself worrying about what others think of you, remember the Twenty-Forty-Sixty Rule: At age twenty, you worry about what others think about you; at forty, you don't care what others think about you; and at sixty, you realize that nobody was thinking about you in the first place.

Instead, tell yourself,

> ### *"I understand that she feels comfortable wearing the same dress every day. Sometimes I feel like doing that, too."*

Empathizing with your child's desire to wear the same clothes will help her know that you understand her fears about letting go of her favorite outfit.

Talking to Your Child

Don't threaten. Don't say,

> ### *"Go ahead and wear that dirty thing. People won't like you if you're dirty."*

Threatening your preschooler with social isolation will have little impact on her. She simply wants to do her own thing. Besides, you want your child to wear clean clothes in order to develop good habits, not because she fears rejection.

Instead, offer other options. Say,

> **"I'm sorry. That dress has to go in the laundry.**
> **Tomorrow it will be clean and you can wear it again.**
> **Until then, let's pick out something else."**

Being firm while providing other options can help your child learn to delay gratification and be flexible. Letting her choose a different outfit appeals to her desire to exert control over what she wears.

Don't belittle. Don't say,

> **"What's the matter with you?**
> **All you want to wear is that dirty old dress."**

Berating your child teaches her that she may lose your love and support because she wants to wear the same dress. Don't make her choose between your love and her dress.

Instead, make a deal. Say,

> **"I understand that you want to wear that dress again today,**
> **but you can't because it's dirty. Let's choose something else to wear.**
> **When you have a different outfit on, then we can watch**
> **your favorite program until it's time to go to school."**

Using Grandma's Rule to motivate your child to choose another outfit can help her learn to make transitions. Grandma's Rule teaches her that when she does what she needs to do, she gets to do what she wants to do.

Don't beg. Don't say,

> **"Please put on the clean dress. Do it for Mommy."**

As tempting as it may be, begging won't teach your child to choose appropriately on her own. Instead, it will teach her to worry about whether you still love her if she doesn't cooperate.

Instead, use empathy. Say,

> **"I know you love your favorite dress. I love mine, too. Let's wash**
> **them together, and we can both wear them when they're clean."**

By empathizing with your child's desire to wear the same clothes, you're letting her know that you're on the same team. Working together will bring you both the results you want.

Chapter Fourteen

"Please Get Dressed Now."
"No! I Don't Wanna Get Dressed!"

When your three-year-old refuses to get dressed after you've repeatedly asked him to do so, he probably has one of several agendas: wanting to decide what to wear, wanting to control when he gets dressed, or wanting to continue what he's doing without interruption. This power struggle can end in disaster unless you stay calm and focus on the goal: getting out the door on time without tears.

Helpful Hints

✋ Before asking your child to get dressed, talk about the type of clothing he'll need to wear that day. This will get him thinking about the routine and will help him choose appropriately.

✋ Make sure your child can perform the tasks required to dress himself. Encourage him to ask for help with tasks he can't manage alone.

✋ Leave enough time to perform dressing and other routines so your child can learn to cooperate without unnecessary pressure.

✋ Make a rule about when your child needs to be dressed in the morning.

Self-Talk

Don't tell yourself,
   "He makes me late every day because he won't get dressed."
Blaming your child for your lateness won't teach him to cooperate.

Instead, tell yourself,
   "I can manage my child's refusal to get dressed."
Affirming your ability to cope with your child's resistance gives you the energy to solve the problem.

Don't tell yourself,

> *"I can't take him to preschool in his pajamas.*
> *His teacher will think I'm a bad parent."*

Worrying about what others may think of you will prevent you from solving the problem. It'll also keep you trying to anticipate what to do so you can please others.

Instead, tell yourself,

> *"I sometimes want to stay in my pj's all day, too."*

Getting dressed makes no sense to preschoolers who are comfy in their jammies. Empathizing with your child helps keep the tone positive so you can figure out creative ways to get him dressed.

Don't tell yourself,

> *"I know he can dress himself. He's just being stubborn like his father."*

Labeling your child as stubborn creates a self-fulfilling prophecy, and blaming someone for your child's behavior may alienate him from that person.

Instead, tell yourself,

> *"It's important for me to avoid creating battle lines over getting dressed."*

Make yourself your child's helper, not his adversary. Doing so will create positive, uplifting feelings as you work together to complete the task.

Talking to Your Child

Don't threaten. Don't say,

> *"If you aren't dressed by the time I come back, you'll get a spanking."*

Threatening physical pain only shows children that parents are bigger and stronger and are willing to hurt them to get their way. Threatening may motivate your child to cooperate in the short term, but you'll get better long-term results if you teach positive behavior rather than punishing your child for disagreeing with you.

Instead, play a game. Say,

> *"Sweetheart, it's time to get dressed. Let's see if you can get your*
> *pants on before the timer rings."*

This kind of contest excites your child and brings out his competitive nature. It motivates him to play the game and beat the timer, forgetting that the game is about getting dressed.

Don't use anger. Don't say,

> *"You're making me mad, so you'd better*
> *get dressed before I really go crazy."*

Using anger to motivate your child gives him power over your feelings, diminishes his ability to empathize, and fails to teach him how to get the job done.

Instead, provide choices. Say,

> *"We need to get dressed now. You can dress yourself,*
> *or I can help dress you. You choose."*

This form of "let's make a deal" tells your child that getting dressed is nonnegotiable, but it offers him choices on how he can complete the task. In this way, both of your agendas are met.

Don't belittle. Don't say,

> *"What's wrong with you? I'm not raising you to be lazy!*
> *Now get in there and get dressed!"*

Implying that your child has a character flaw may make him think he can't achieve goals, is unworthy of his parents' love, and is helpless to change his behavior.

Instead, be helpful. Say,

> *"I'll help you with your shoes and socks when*
> *you've put your pants and shirt on."*

Offering to do part of the task can motivate your child to do the rest. Working as partners teaches him that teamwork can get the job done.

Don't bribe. Don't say,

> *"If you get yourself dressed, I'll buy you a treat on the way to school."*

Bribing encourages your child to hold out for a reward before he cooperates. Giving him the "if" option tempts him to think, "What if I don't?" He may refuse to cooperate just to see what you'll do.

Instead, make a deal. Say,

> *"When you have your clothes on, then we can have breakfast together."*

It's your job to teach your child that doing what's necessary comes before doing what he wants. Using Grandma's Rule will give him a healthy incentive to cooperate.

Don't nag. Don't say,

> **"I've asked you five times to get dressed!**
> **How many more times will it take?"**

Nagging your child will teach him that he doesn't have to listen because you don't follow through with consequences.

Instead, remind him about the rule. Say,

> **"The rule is that we get dressed before we play."**

This makes the *rule* the enforcer and frees you to act as your child's helper.

Chapter Fifteen

"Please Put On Your Shoes." "No! I Don't Wanna Wear Shoes!"

For some two-year-olds, wearing no shoes is the ultimate joy. Demanding that they wear shoes can spark a meltdown. Explain to your child that the ground or floor is sometimes dangerous (broken glass, splinters, sharp rocks, hot asphalt, and so on) so she understands that covering her feet will protect her. Meanwhile, let her run around barefoot whenever it's safe to do so.

Helpful Hints

✋ Establish rules about when and where shoes must be worn for safety and social reasons.

✋ Model appropriate behavior by talking about what footwear you're wearing and why. For example, "I'm wearing my boots today because it's cold and wet outside."

✋ Let the thermometer and weather forecast dictate when footwear should be worn.

✋ Make sure your child has the dexterity to put her shoes on before demanding that she do so.

Self-Talk

Don't tell yourself,
**"She'll never learn to put her shoes on.
She'll be walking around in bare feet for the rest of her life."**
Thinking that your child will *never* learn to do something exaggerates the problem. Assuming a hopeless, helpless attitude diminishes your willingness to find creative solutions.

Instead, tell yourself,

> ***"She'll learn to put her shoes on eventually.***
> ***In the meantime, I can help her."***

Keeping a positive attitude about your child's development prevents you from having unrealistic expectations about her abilities. In addition, keeping an open mind helps you be creative. For example, you might have her try Velcro shoes instead of shoes with laces.

Don't tell yourself,

> ***"The neighbors will think we're bad parents if she doesn't***
> ***wear shoes, so she has to wear them no matter what."***

Don't make parenting decisions based on what others may think of you. You're the most qualified person to make decisions about your child's safety and happiness.

Instead, tell yourself,

> ***"The reason I want her to wear shoes is for her own safety."***

Keep in mind the reasoning behind your rule, and keep focused on the goal when your child tests the rule.

Talking to Your Child

Don't threaten. Don't say,

> ***"You'll get those shoes on NOW if you know what's good for you!"***

Vague threats are not only poor motivators, they teach your child that it's okay to use fear to control others.

Instead, remind her about the rule. Say,

> ***"What's the rule about wearing shoes? What does the thermometer say?"***

Reminding your child of the rule will help her learn to monitor the weather conditions before deciding what to wear. The rule becomes her guide and nemesis—not you.

Don't use anger. Don't say,

> ***"I'm starting to get mad,***
> ***so you better get those shoes on before I get really mad!"***

Don't use anger to motivate your child. Doing so makes her fearful and diminishes her ability to empathize. It also squanders the opportunity to teach her that teamwork and cooperation are good for both of you.

Instead, practice. Say,

> *"Let's practice putting on your shoes.*
> *I'll help you get them on and you can do the straps."*

Practicing a new skill is important for mastery. Work on it together one step at a time, and praise her progress generously.

Don't bribe. Don't say,

> *"If you put your shoes on, I'll give you some candy."*

Bribing your child tells her that she can hold out for a reward before cooperating. Don't set up a system in which doing what you ask requires a reward.

Instead, make a deal. Say,

> *"When you have your shoes on, then we can go to the park*
> *like you wanted. Sometimes there are sharp objects on the ground*
> *at the park, so the rule says you have to wear shoes."*

Grandma's Rule motivates your child to cooperate so she can do what she wants to do, and your explanation for the rule reinforces the importance of following it.

Chapter Sixteen

"Let's Put On This Shirt."
"No! I Don't Wanna Wear That!"

How would you feel if someone told you what to wear every day? The ultimate goal of a three-year-old is to control his world, so get ready for his opinions to matter more to him than your dress code. To avoid a battle and teach your little one how to choose clothing appropriately, make rules about the kind of clothing that will be worn for different occasions and weather conditions.

Helpful Hints

✋ Work with your child to choose outfits ahead of time to prevent delays when you're in a hurry. Be willing to stick to your mutual decision if battles flare up later. Otherwise, your child will learn to test all your decisions, whether they were mutual or not.

✋ Encourage your child's eye for coordination by arranging matching outfits in different drawers or containers.

✋ If necessary, wean your child slowly from his favorite article of clothing by restricting him from wearing it one day the first week, two days the second, and so on until he wears it only one day a week or less often.

Self-Talk

Don't tell yourself,

"What's the matter with my child?
He's always so particular about his clothes."

Avoid putting a negative spin on a neutral fact of life. There's nothing "wrong" with your child wanting to wear something he really likes.

Instead, tell yourself,

"I'm glad my child has opinions and is willing to express them."

Respecting your child's opinions will help you learn to work together as a team.

Don't tell yourself,

> *"He'd better shape up. His pickiness is making me crazy."*

Allowing your child's behavior to control how you feel is irrational and counterproductive.

Instead, tell yourself,

> *"Just because he has a mind of his own doesn't mean I have to get upset. Instead, I should nurture and guide his independence."*

Letting your child make decisions within established limits will validate his opinions. Giving him limited control will show him that he can make decisions and be a team player, too.

Don't tell yourself,

> *"He's as bullheaded as his father (or mother), and I can't stand having two of them living in my house."*

Although a stubborn streak may seem to run in your family, telling yourself that you hate it undermines your ability to cope and creates anger and resentment toward your child's other parent.

Instead, tell yourself,

> *"Just because he's being rigid doesn't mean he has a problem."*

Keep the situation in perspective. Focus on what's appropriate to wear in certain circumstances, not on your child's character.

Talking to Your Child

Don't belittle. Don't say,

> *"What's the matter with you?*
> *Why can't you just wear what you're supposed to wear?"*

Implying that your child is flawed squelches his healthy desire to express his opinions. Also, asking a "why" question may make him defensive in order to justify his position.

Instead, teach the rule. Say,

> *"I know you want to wear swim trunks to school,*
> *but the rule says that we wear pants and shirts to school.*
> *You may wear swim trunks when you get home."*

Invoking the rule takes the pressure off you being the "bad guy" and gives your child options to choose from, within the permitted range.

Don't use anger. Don't say,

> **"Just put on what I tell you!**
> **I'm sick and tired of your wanting to wear weird things!"**

Although you may be tempted to react with anger when you're frustrated, think of how your child would feel on the receiving end of such verbal abuse.

Instead, use empathy. Say,

> **"I know you want to wear shorts today.**
> **I'd like to wear shorts, too. But the rule is that we wear pants and long-sleeve shirts when the thermometer says it's cold outside."**

Showing your child that you empathize with his desire to wear his favorite clothes tells him that you care about his opinions. Letting the rule dictate what clothing is appropriate gives your child the freedom to make decisions within established guidelines. In addition, it teaches him that rules govern our behavior by telling us what's appropriate.

Don't beg. Don't say,

> **"Come on, sweetheart, wear what Mommy wants."**

Begging your child tells him that he's in control, a prospect that usually frightens children. In addition, using guilt to motivate his cooperation inspires him to do what you ask because he wants to make sure you still love him. He shouldn't perceive your love as dependent on his willingness to cooperate.

Instead, remind him about the rule. Say,

> **"I know you want to wear shorts today.**
> **Does the thermometer say it's warm enough for shorts?"**

Making the thermometer the enforcer reduces potential conflict with you. It also teaches your child how to monitor weather conditions to make appropriate decisions.

Chapter Seventeen

"Please Change Your Clothes."
"No! I Don't Wanna Change My Clothes!"

When your five-year-old protests changing into party clothes or her soccer uniform, she's letting you know that she believes her dress code should be *her* choice. In fact, she believes *everything* should be her choice! So decide when clothing rules should apply (because of weather, safety concerns, social courtesies, cleanliness, or comfort) and when they shouldn't.

Helpful Hints

- 🖐 Whenever possible, tell your child why you're changing your clothes, so she can learn when and why certain clothing is appropriate.

- 🖐 Minimize your child's clothing options to avoid confusion and meltdowns. For example, say, "You may choose to change into your jeans or overalls before going outside to play."

Self-Talk

Don't tell yourself,

> *"Why can't she get it through her head that she needs to change into play clothes when she wants to go outside with her friends?"*

Wearing appropriate clothing isn't a high priority for a preschooler.

Instead, tell yourself,

> *"My job is to help my child learn to follow the rules."*

Helping your child learn when to change clothes will reinforce the larger lesson that rules provide the framework for appropriate behavior. Knowing the rules will reduce her anxiety about not knowing what to do.

Don't tell yourself,

"My mother warned me that I'd have a bad kid, and she was right."

Just because your child resists changing clothes doesn't make her a bad person. Using your mother's admonition to explain your child's lack of cooperation will only increase your frustration; it won't help you solve the problem.

Instead, tell yourself,

"My child's resistance to change is normal. I can handle it."

Understanding that children—and adults—often resist change will help you cope with your child's behavior.

Don't tell yourself,

"She never listens to me. Why can't she just do what she's told?"

Exaggerating the situation with absolute terms like *always* or *never* prevents you from understanding your child's behavior and solving the problem.

Instead, tell yourself,

"Her resistance doesn't mean that she'll never learn to listen."

Empathizing with your child's need to have some control over her life will help you teach her how to make decisions as she grows up.

Talking to Your Child

Don't belittle. Don't say,

"No, you can't wear that! Are you crazy?"

Implying that your child has a mental problem won't motivate her to comply, but it will set the stage for a poor self-image. It will also teach her to judge others and use harsh words to describe their behavior.

Instead, remind her about the rule. Say,

"What's the rule about what you're supposed to wear to soccer practice?"

Reminding her of the rule reinforces it in her mind and puts it in control of the situation. You become her helper, not her adversary.

Don't beg. Don't say,

> *"Why can't you just be a good girl and change your clothes?"*

Begging your child to be a "good girl" commits two costly errors: It implies that something is wrong with her because she doesn't want to change her clothes, and it doesn't separate her from her behavior. Since your child's behavior doesn't define who she is, avoid phrases like "good girl" and "bad girl."

Instead, make a deal. Say,

> *"When you've changed into your play clothes, then you may go outside with the other kids."*

This use of Grandma's Rule tells your child that she has choices and that her choices have consequences. She's free to choose not to change her clothes (and give up playing with her friends) or she can do what you've asked and get what she wants.

Don't threaten. Don't say,

> *"If you don't change your clothes, I'm going to get mad. You don't want me to get mad, do you?"*

Daring your child to make you mad gives her two unattractive choices: She may refuse to cooperate just to watch you explode (an exciting lesson in cause and effect), or she may choose to cooperate out of fear.

Instead, reframe the situation. Say,

> *"Since tomorrow is Saturday, you won't have to put on school clothes when you get up. But today's a school day, so let's get dressed for school."*

Giving your child something to look forward to may distract her from her desire to stay in the clothes she's wearing.

Don't nag. Don't say,

> *"How many times do I have to tell you to change your clothes?"*

Nagging doesn't teach your child to cooperate and offers no motivation for her to follow your directions.

Instead, play a game. Say,

> *"Let's see if you can get changed into your dress clothes before the timer rings."*

Using your child's natural competitive spirit distracts her from the emerging confrontation and playfully motivates her to cooperate.

SECTION III
EATING

I think the next best thing to solving a
problem is finding some humor in it.

—*Frank Clark*

Chapter Eighteen

"Please Stay at the Table."
"No! I Wanna Get Down!"

This plea to leave the table is a family classic. Once your four-year-old is full, he's no longer interested in table talk and thinks it's time to play elsewhere. Be realistic about the amount of time you expect him to chat and chew—and how long that time feels to a little one who has a much shorter attention span than you.

Helpful Hints

🖐 Turn off the TV and computer during meals so they don't distract your child from eating.

🖐 Set a timer to tell your child when it's okay for him to leave the table.

🖐 If necessary, make sure someone can supervise your child when he leaves the table, so you'll know he's safe before sending him off.

🖐 Try eating as many meals as possible sitting at the table, so your child becomes used to it. Limit eating in the car and elsewhere.

Self-Talk

Don't tell yourself,

"Now that I'm divorced, I'll never be able to give my child the wonderful family meals I remember from my childhood."

Using words like *never* and *always* will make you feel helpless to change your circumstances or redefine your perspective. Just because you're divorced doesn't mean you can't have family meals.

Instead, tell yourself,
"Having my child eat meals with me is still a family experience."
Even though both parents can't be at the dinner table, recognizing the importance of eating meals with your child will help him develop a sense of family togetherness. Keep these experiences pleasant by not nagging your child to stay at the table beyond a reasonable time.

Don't tell yourself,
"My child doesn't like my company at the table."
Don't take your child's desire to leave the table personally. Remember, his main agenda is to get down and play, not sit still with grownups.

Instead, tell yourself,
"Talking to my child during meals is important, even if it's for just a few minutes."
Measure your table time in terms of its quality, not quantity. It's not the length of time at the table; it's the amount of fun and love you share there.

Don't tell yourself,
"My child's screaming to get down is ruining dinner for the rest of us."
Telling yourself you can't cope with your child's noise doesn't help you do so and doesn't teach him to enjoy mealtime with his family. Remember, all events are neutral; dinner is "ruined" only if you choose to think of it that way.

Instead, tell yourself,
"Even though I'm tired after a long day at work, sitting down to dinner together is important."
Reaffirm how significant family meals are to your child's development. Even if dinner time is loud, messy, and wild when you'd rather have calm at the end of a frenzied workday, it's important for strengthening family connections.

Talking to Your Child

Don't threaten. Don't say,

"If you don't stay at the table, you'll have to go to bed.
You don't want that, do you?"

Threatening isolation for wanting to get down and play won't teach your child to enjoy the family meal. Plus, it will associate his bed with punishment. It may also challenge him to call your bluff by thinking, "What if I don't stay at the table? Will she follow through?"

Instead, praise cooperative behavior. Say,

"Thank you for sitting so nicely at the table. We love your company."

Everyone wants to be appreciated. Praising your child's patience, however fleeting it might be, will encourage him to be even more patient the next time.

Don't force. Don't say,

"You're going to sit at the table until your plate is clean."

Forcing your child to "make a happy plate" teaches him to continue eating after he feels full, which can lead to eating disorders and childhood obesity. You want him to learn to respond to his body's hunger cues, so don't force him to overeat.

Instead, play a game. Say,

"Let's play the good-day game.
Each of us can tell about a good thing that happened today."

Encourage your child to stay at the table by asking him to tell a story about something fun that happened to him that day. Not only will he like telling his own stories, he'll enjoy hearing other stories.

Don't bribe. Don't say,

"If you stay at the table a little longer, I'll get you some ice cream."

Getting a reward for doing what you've asked teaches your child that his cooperation comes with a price.

Instead, remind him about the rule. Say,

"I know you want to get down from the table,
but the rule says that you may get down when the timer rings."

By showing empathy and encouragement while invoking the rule, you'll increase your child's resilience and help him understand that rules help us navigate our world.

Chapter Nineteen

"Please Use Your Fork (or Spoon)."
"No! I Don't Wanna Use a Fork!"

"Why use a fork when my fingers work just fine?" "Why use a napkin when my shirt is handy?" This is the thinking of a three-year-old who isn't as interested in table manners as you are. Model acceptable eating behavior, and encourage your child to follow your lead so one day she'll be comfortable dining with kids or kings!

Helpful Hints

❦ Make rules about table manners and compliment your child for following them.

❦ Model appropriate table manners, and point out what you're doing. For example, say, "I'm putting my napkin in my lap and picking up my fork."

❦ Avoid serving finger foods too often (such as burgers, fries, and pizza) so your child can get plenty of practice using a fork and spoon.

❦ Have your child help set the table occasionally, and talk about how to use napkins and utensils.

Self-Talk

Don't tell yourself,
> "She'll never learn to use a fork, so I might as well give up."

Don't play the helpless, hopeless card. It doesn't teach your child how to use manners, and it will only upset you every time you remind her about the rule.

Instead, tell yourself,
> "I need to stay calm and continue to teach
> her how to use manners at the table."

Keep the problem in perspective by not making a big deal about it. Your patience will eventually pay off. Your child's motivation to use good manners will increase when she knows you still respect her when her manners aren't perfect.

Don't tell yourself,

> *"Her father doesn't encourage her to use manners in his home,*
> *so she refuses to use them in mine. It makes me crazy!"*

Don't make your child or your child's other parent responsible for your feelings. Take control of your feelings by choosing how to react.

Instead, tell yourself,

> *"I can only encourage good manners in my home.*
> *I can't control what happens elsewhere."*

Concentrate on what your child does in your home to help you feel more in control of the situation.

Don't tell yourself,

> *"I hate the mess my child makes when she eats like a pig."*

Don't feel sorry for yourself because you have to clean up after your child. Young kids are messy sometimes, and cleaning up is part of your job description. Accepting an occasional mess will keep your stress level down and will help you teach your child appropriate eating habits.

Instead, tell yourself,

> *"I don't need to feel guilty because my child*
> *doesn't want to use good manners at the table."*

Children aren't born with good manners; the learning process takes time and patience.

Talking to Your Child

Don't threaten. Don't say,

> *"If you pick up one more thing with your fingers,*
> *I'm going to smack you. Now use your fork."*

Never threaten physical violence. Doing so only teaches your child that you're bigger and stronger and willing to inflict pain to get her to follow directions. Violence isn't necessary when teaching appropriate behavior.

Instead, remind her about the rule. Say,

> *"What's the rule about using a fork instead of your fingers?*
> *I know you want to follow the rule."*

Expect your child to follow the rule, but let her know that you're on her side. Be her coach, not her dictator.

Don't nag. Don't say,

> *"How many times do I have to tell you not to eat with your fingers?"*

Constant admonitions suggest that your child is somehow mentally deficient, and they tell her what *not* to do rather than what to do. Focus on the positive so you can encourage the behavior you want.

Instead, be supportive. Say,

> *"I know learning to hold a fork is hard. Remember how you hold a pencil? That's how you hold a fork. Now let's try again."*

Gentle coaching helps your child learn difficult skills and models patience.

Don't use putdowns. Don't say,

> *"Having food on your chin is so disgusting, I don't even want to look at you."*

Don't suggest that your child is acceptable only when she's doing what you ask. Doing so sends her the message that your love is conditional and will disappear if she doesn't behave the way you want.

Instead, praise cooperative behavior. Say,

> *"Thank you for remembering to use your napkin. That shows good manners."*

Praising your child's behavior when she uses good manners tells her they're important and encourages her to continue using them. Everyone is motivated to cooperate when cooperation is praised.

Don't bribe. Don't say,

> *"If you use your fork, I'll let you have some ice cream for dessert."*

Bribing your child to use manners doesn't motivate her to use them because it's the acceptable thing to do. It motivates her to expect a reward for her cooperation.

Instead, make a deal. Say,

> *"When you use your fork, you can stay at the table. Otherwise, dinner will be over and you'll have to get down."*

In this case, Grandma's Rule not only conveys the importance of using manners, it gives your child a choice between using manners and ending her meal.

Chapter Twenty

"Please Eat What's on Your Plate."
"No! I Don't Wanna Eat That!"

Mealtimes can be stressful when a toddler's agenda collides with a parent's. Don't let your child's eating habits induce a power struggle. Remember that healthy children eat when they're hungry and stop eating when they're full. If you're worried about the quality or quantity of the food your child eats, keep a record for a few weeks (writing down when, where, and what he eats). This information will help you and your child's healthcare provider evaluate the situation.

Helpful Hints

🖐 Don't try to force your child to eat a big meal when he isn't hungry, such as shortly after a snack or drink.

🖐 It's normal for children to be less cooperative when they're hungry or tired. Consider that your child may be cranky when he doesn't want to eat what he's served.

🖐 Be aware of the recommended nutrition guidelines for toddlers and preschoolers. Contact the National Dairy Council at 847-803-2000 or check their website at www.nutritionexplorations.org.

Self-Talk

Don't tell yourself,

"If he doesn't eat, he'll die."

Don't exaggerate the consequences of your child's occasional refusal to eat what you serve. Doing so will only upset you. However, if he stops eating altogether or changes his eating habits drastically, consult your healthcare provider.

Instead, tell yourself,

> *"My child won't starve if he misses a meal once in a while or if he doesn't always eat his vegetables."*

Understand that occasionally refusing food won't adversely affect your child's overall health. Once you calm down about his eating habits, you can think creatively about ways to motivate him to eat those veggies.

Don't tell yourself,

> *"I expect my child to clean his plate like I had to when I was a kid."*

Pressuring your child to continue eating when he's full may put him at risk for eating disorders and childhood obesity.

Instead, tell yourself,

> *"Making a 'happy plate' isn't important. What's important is that my child feels comfortable at mealtime."*

Creating a calm, supportive environment will make eating an enjoyable, nourishing experience for everyone involved.

Don't tell yourself,

> *"I feel rejected when my child won't eat what I make."*

Dismantle this old parenting land mine once and for all. Taking your child's behavior personally won't help the situation.

Instead, tell yourself,

> *"My child's refusal to eat has nothing to do with me."*

Your child is rejecting the food, not you. Separating the two is essential in helping him establish a healthy attitude toward eating.

Talking to Your Child

Don't demand. Don't say,

> *"You're going to sit there until you've eaten everything on your plate."*

Forcing your child to eat after he's had enough can lead to overeating and obesity. As with other aspects of his behavior, trying to control his eating habits is futile and counterproductive.

Instead, offer choices. Say,

> *"I see you've had enough to eat. You may get down and play, or you can sit here and talk to us while we finish."*

When your child starts to play with his food, chances are he's had enough. Removing his plate or allowing him to leave the table will prevent the situation from escalating into a food fight.

Don't use guilt. Don't say,

> *"Now, sweetheart, you know Mommy worked really hard to fix this food. Please eat my food."*

Associating food with love is a sure-fire way to promote an eating disorder. Don't encourage your child to think, "If I don't eat Mommy's food, she'll think I don't love her."

Instead, encourage communication. Say,

> *"When you're done with your food, say 'All done.' Then I'll help you get down."*

Encouraging your child to tell you when he's finished lets him exert needed control over his world.

Don't back him into a corner. Don't say,

> *"Too bad you don't like what we're having. You can eat it or leave the table. If you leave, I don't want to hear any whining about being hungry because you're not getting anything else to eat."*

Your lack of empathy will show your child that you don't care about his feelings, which will only increase his anger and defiance.

Instead, use empathy. Say,

> *"I'm sorry you don't want to eat what we're having. Our tastes change sometimes, so I want you to taste this to see if you like it now."*

Empathizing with your child will encourage him to taste a food he may have previously rejected. It'll also help him try new foods he may have otherwise rejected on sight.

SECTION IV
MANNERS

Guard well within yourself that treasure, kindness.
Know how to give without hesitation, how to lose
without regret, how to acquire without meanness.

—George Sand

Chapter Twenty-one

"Please Let Your Brother Watch His Show." "No! I Wanna Watch My Show!"

Battles over the TV remote can start early. Since your five-year-old probably understands the power that's associated with that little device, make rules about what TV shows she can and cannot watch—and when.

Helpful Hints

✋ Monitor your own behavior when sharing the remote and other entertainment devices. Your children will learn from your example.

✋ Limit your TV viewing so your child won't get the message that watching lots of TV is okay.

Self-Talk

Don't tell yourself,

"I just want to scream when my kids fight over the TV."

Telling yourself that you're at the end of your rope impedes your ability to cope with sibling rivalry.

Instead, tell yourself,

"This teachable moment will help my children learn how to get along."

Looking for the teachable moment during conflicts will keep you focused on your role as educator for your little ones.

Don't tell yourself,

"Why can't they share their things? I should never have had two kids."

Don't blame yourself for your children's disputes over shared space and belongings.

Instead, tell yourself,
>*"It's not possible for my kids to get along all the time."*

Occasional sibling conflict is a normal part of family life. When you accept this fact, you can calmly respond to your children's behavior without taking it personally. Teach your children how to resolve their differences in a safe, nurturing environment in which everyone is valued and respected.

Don't tell yourself,
>*"She's so selfish. I can't stand selfish children."*

Labeling your child as selfish makes the label a permanent part of who she is, which will discourage you from teaching her how to cooperate.

Instead, tell yourself,
>*"My job is to help my child learn to be a team player."*

Lessons in cooperation, collaboration, and compromise will bring out your child's innate capacity for empathy and sharing.

Talking to Your Child

Don't give in. Don't say,
>*"Okay, I guess it's your turn. Go ahead and change the channel if you want."*

Giving in won't teach your child to cooperate and share with others. It will only tell her that she can get her way if she pushes hard enough for it. If your other child is competing for TV time, giving in will only anger the sibling who believes he was treated unfairly.

Instead, make a deal. Say,
>*"When you take turns watching your shows, you may continue to watch. Otherwise, the TV will have to be turned off."*

Grandma's Rule, which teaches that duty comes before pleasure, will encourage sharing as your children look to the long-term benefits of compromise.

Don't shame. Don't say,
>*"You're so selfish. Why can't you share?"*

Telling your child that she's selfish suggests that her selfishness is an insurmountable character flaw, which gives her permission to continue to behave selfishly.

Instead, remind her about the rule. Say,
"What's the rule about sharing the remote?"
Asking your child to state the rule ensures her knowledge of it and reminds her that it will be enforced. When you've established the rule as the authority, you can then be on your child's side in encouraging her to follow it.

Don't bribe. Don't say,
"If you share the remote, I'll give you some candy."
Bribing your child teaches her that she can get a reward for cooperating—and that she should continue resisting your request until she gets an offer.

Instead, be a role model. Say,
"See how Mommy and Daddy share the TV? We take turns when we both want to watch! I hope you can share like that, too, when you're at your friend's house."
Modeling appropriate behavior helps your child learn to share. Using the words and body language associated with sharing (smiling, saying please and thank you, and so on) will encourage her to imitate those actions.

Don't lecture. Don't say,
"I'm going to explain to you once and for all why we have to share the TV. Now listen!"
Lecturing actually discourages your child from listening because she tunes out after a short time. Chances are she knows what the rule is, but since you haven't done anything to enforce it, she doesn't need to take it seriously.

Instead, offer consequences. Say,
"I'm sorry you've chosen not to share the remote. The TV will have to be turned off now."
Empathize with your child while following through with consequences when she violates rules. Tell her that you're sorry she made inappropriate decisions, but you meant what you said. This will enhance your credibility and increase the chances of her choosing to cooperate next time.

Chapter Twenty-two

"Please Say Thank You."
"No! I Don't Wanna Say Thank You!"

Many parents cringe when their three-year-old refuses to say thank you after a friend gives him a birthday gift or a grandparent offers him a cookie. Your job is to teach good manners; your child's job is to practice them until they become a habit. Model the behavior you want your child to use as you teach him the rule about speaking to people with courtesy and respect. To encourage courteous behavior in a world that's often rude and crude, ask your child to tell you the manners rules and praise his use of them.

Helpful Hints

🖐 Modeling good manners not only shows your child how they work, it confirms their importance.

🖐 Establishing rules about manners will set positive guidelines your child can use when dealing with others.

Self-Talk

Don't tell yourself,
> *"He's such a rude child. I'm afraid no one will like him."*

Don't label your child as rude just because he isn't using his manners yet. Simply continue to encourage mannerly behavior, and make sure to model it whenever possible.

Instead, tell yourself,
> *"Just because he forgets to say please and thank you doesn't mean he'll grow up to be a rude adult."*

Realize that your child is young and still learning important life lessons. Keep a positive attitude about the future, and don't assume that his behavior at three will be the same at twenty-three.

Don't tell yourself,

"He'll never learn to say please and thank you like the other kids."

Comparing your child to other children can be dangerous, unless you're looking at growth charts. Exaggerating your child's lack of manners by saying he'll *never* learn them—and feeling embarrassed because he hasn't—are unproductive ways of dealing with the problem.

Instead, tell yourself,

"My child's refusal to use manners means I still need to work with him."

Your job as a teaching parent is to help your child learn manners. When he doesn't want to use them, you need to find out what thoughts and feelings might be influencing his behavior.

Don't tell yourself,

"I'm so embarrassed when he's rude. How many times do I have to tell him to say hello to our neighbors?"

Telling yourself that your child's lack of manners is embarrassing will only increase your guilt and prevent you from finding effective ways of teaching him these valuable lessons. You're embarrassed because you believe his lack of manners reflects poorly on you as a parent. Remember, you can only *teach* your child these lessons; he's ultimately responsible for putting them to use.

Instead, tell yourself,

"Other parents understand the difficulty preschoolers have in remembering to say please and thank you."

Remember that your experience is not unique. Find comfort in the fact that teaching young children appropriate behavior is challenging for every parent. Continue to remind your child that using good manners will result in positive attention from friends and family.

Talking to Your Child

Don't label. Don't say,

"Why are you so rude?"

First of all, your child may have no idea what *rude* means. If he does, referring to him this way may make him believe it's an unchangeable part of his personality.

Instead, use praise. Say,

> *"That was polite of you to say thank you to your friend.*
> *I'm sure he appreciated it."*

Praising your child's use of manners increases the chance that he'll repeat the behavior. Don't forget to point out how grateful people are when manners are used.

Don't use guilt. Don't say,

> *"You embarrassed me when you didn't say hello to Mrs. Jones.*
> *What am I going to do with you?"*

Don't tell your child that he embarrasses you. That tells him that he's responsible for your feelings.

Instead, practice. Say,

> *"What do we say when someone gives us something?*
> *Let's practice before we go to Grandma's.*
> *She always gives you cookies when we're there,*
> *and she really likes it when you say thank you."*

Asking about the rule and practicing it ahead of time keeps manners fresh in your child's mind and improves the odds that he'll use them when the time comes.

Don't threaten. Don't say,

> *"If you don't say thank you to Grandma when*
> *she gives you a cookie, I'll have to swat you and*
> *put you in time-out. Now remember that."*

Threatening physical violence and isolation won't teach your child to use manners. It will only show him that if you're bigger and stronger, you can intimidate people to do what you want.

Instead, make a deal. Say,

> *"When you say please, then you may have a cookie."*

This most basic use of Grandma's Rule tells your child that when he follows the manners rules, he gets the results he wants.

Chapter Twenty-three

"Please Be Quiet."
"No! I Don't Wanna Be Quiet!"

Curious two-year-olds are notorious for testing parents' resolve when they're told to be quiet. Some even take the opportunity to see what happens if they use a *louder* voice! Teach your child the rule about using a quiet voice by role-playing the behavior before it's actually needed in church, synagogue, the library, and so on. Tell her that certain tones of voice are used out of respect for others. This lesson in empathy turns a potentially explosive situation into a teachable moment, motivating your child to cooperate because she cares about others' feelings.

Helpful Hints

☝ Use animal references to help your child remember when and where she can use different voices. For example, ask her to be "quiet as a mouse" in church, and to "roar like a lion" at soccer.

☝ If your child is a habitually loud talker, have her hearing checked to make sure she doesn't have hearing loss.

☝ Before taking your child to an event that requires being quiet, consider her ability to understand and enjoy the event.

Self-Talk

Don't tell yourself,
"I must make her stay quiet when she's supposed to."
Understand that you can't *make* your child do anything. You can only teach her the skills and reinforce them whenever possible.

Instead, tell yourself,
"It's okay that she can't remember to be quiet every time we're in church. We'll keep working on it until she can remember."
Teaching positive behaviors takes time. Be prepared to stick with the task as long as necessary.

Don't tell yourself,

"I refuse to take her out anymore because she's always so loud."

This overreaction focuses on the problem of using a loud voice rather than on the solution of teaching her to use a quiet voice.

Instead, tell yourself,

"Just because she's loud doesn't mean she can't learn to be quiet."

You can't control your child's behavior, so don't feel guilty and embarrassed when she makes mistakes or occasionally forgets the rule. Simply take it in stride and remind her of the appropriate behavior.

Don't tell yourself,

"If people get upset because she's talking too loudly in the movie theater, they can just move."

Don't make others responsible for coping with your child's loudness in a theater or restaurant. This models disrespect for others and prevents your child from learning to use her quiet voice.

Instead, tell yourself,

"My child might not understand the rule because she hasn't had enough practice."

If you haven't exposed your child to quiet places such as church, synagogue, or the library, take some field trips to help her understand when and why she needs to use her quiet voice.

Talking to Your Child

Don't shame. Don't say,

**"What's the matter with you?
Don't you have any respect for other people?"**

Suggesting that your child is uncaring and unfeeling won't show her how to use her manners. When you treat her with disrespect, it will be hard for her to learn to respect others and will give her permission to continue behaving in a self-centered way.

Instead, remind her about the rule. Say,

"I'm sorry you forgot that we're supposed to use our quiet voice in the library. Next time, I'm sure you'll remember the rule."

Empathizing with your child tells her that you understand how she feels, but that the rule still applies. Reminding her of the rule helps her learn the lesson without putting her down. *She's* still okay; it's her *behavior* that's inappropriate.

Don't threaten. Don't say,

"If you can't be quiet, I'll give you a swat! Now shut up!"

Never physically or verbally abuse your child. These words and actions not only model behavior you don't want your child to use, they also tell her that threatening someone is an acceptable method of getting what you want.

Instead, practice. Say,

"Let's practice using our quiet voice for a while before we go to the library. You know the library has a rule about being quiet."

Practicing is a good way to make sure your child understands the rule. Make practicing fun by smiling as your child uses her quiet voice and telling her how much you like it.

Don't bribe. Don't say,

"I'll give you some candy if you'll whisper instead of talking out loud."

Bribing your child won't teach her to use manners out of respect for others. She'll only do it to get a reward.

Instead, make a deal. Say,

"When you follow the quiet-voice rule, then we'll be able to stay and enjoy the program. Otherwise, we'll have to leave."

Use Grandma's Rule to teach your child that she has choices and that those choices lead to positive and negative consequences. Letting her decide which choice to make helps her feel more in control and gives her practice in making decisions. She also learns that cooperating with your request leads to getting to do what she wants.

Don't belittle. Don't say,

"Nobody likes a big mouth, so just be quiet."

Don't tell your child that she won't be likable because she talks loudly. This won't teach her to use her manners and may lead her to feel like an outcast.

Instead, praise cooperative behavior. Say,

"Thank you for using your quiet voice.
You're following the quiet-voice rule so nicely."

Praising your child for using her quiet voice not only reminds her of the rule but also encourages her to continue being quiet. Children want to cooperate with people they trust and respect—and with people who respect them in return.

Don't nag. Don't say,

"I've asked you three times now to be quiet.
How many times do I have to ask you?"

Nagging your child won't teach her to use a quiet voice out of respect for others. When you nag, you essentially throw up your hands in despair, which accomplishes nothing.

Instead, remind her about the rule. Say,

"We're going to church this morning.
What's the rule about using quiet voices while we're there?"

Ask your child to tell you the rule as a subtle reminder of how to behave in church. When she explains the rule, she feels in charge of the situation and is motivated to follow the rule.

Chapter Twenty-four

"Please Sit Here."
"No! I Don't Wanna Sit There!"

When your five-year-old clashes with you over where to sit in a movie theater, at the dinner table, or in the car, he's letting you know that he's a normal, healthy child who wants to exert some control over what he does and where he does it. Think of his behavior as a positive sign that he wants to make his own choices. So let him—within limits—to give him practice in a skill he'll need his entire life.

Helpful Hint

✋ Make a seating chart for the car, the dinner table, and other places where your child haggles over his seat. This lets him practice taking turns democratically. Discuss the seating arrangement with him ahead of time to avoid squabbles.

Self-Talk

Don't tell yourself,

"It's so stupid for him to care about where he sits."

Don't belittle your child's desire to make his own choices. It's his way of asserting his identity, so support his effort.

Instead, tell yourself,

"Where I sit may not be important to me,
but it's important to him, and I need to respect that."

Empathizing with your child will prevent the situation from escalating into a major conflict. A caring, respectful attitude will help you calmly and patiently obtain his cooperation.

Don't tell yourself,

> *"It makes me so mad when he gets upset over little things."*

Your getting upset over little things teaches your child to follow your example.

Instead, tell yourself,

> *"I don't need to upset myself over my child's desire to control what he does. That's his job as a preschooler."*

Understand your child's developmental level. At this age, he needs to practice sharing his opinions and desires. Support his growing independence!

Don't tell yourself,

> *"He'd better sit where I tell him to sit, because I'm the parent."*

Don't assume the role of dictator. Doing so will teach your child how to give orders but not how to cooperate and compromise, two lessons you want him to learn and practice his entire life.

Instead, tell yourself,

> *"This is an opportunity to teach my child to compromise."*

Think about your response to your child's seating request as a teachable moment. Although you wouldn't mind his simply sitting where you told him to sit, celebrate his healthy sense of self and his ability to express his opinions.

Talking to Your Child

Don't yell. Don't say,

> *"What's the matter with you? You know you can't sit there, so move it!"*

There's nothing wrong with a child who asserts his independence. Your militant approach will create two problems: It will model authoritarian behavior that you don't want him to imitate, and it will make him reluctant to express his feelings for fear you'll yell at him.

Instead, remind him about the rule. Say,

> *"What's the rule about sitting in the car?*
> *When you follow the rule, you'll be safe."*

Safety must be your primary consideration. Asking your child to repeat the rule reminds him to follow it.

Don't bribe. Don't say,

> *"If you sit in the back seat, where you're supposed to sit,*
> *we can stop at the store and buy you a treat."*

Bribing your child to follow the seating rules only tells him that he can get a reward for doing what he's supposed to do. You want him to learn to follow the rule because it's the safe thing to do.

Instead, empathize. Say,

> *"I'm sorry you can't sit there. I know you want to sit up front,*
> *but the back seat is the safe seat for children."*

Empathizing with your child's desire to choose his seat shows him how to empathize with others and helps him understand why he must follow the car-seat rule.

Don't threaten. Don't say,

> *"If you don't get in the seat you're supposed to be in,*
> *I'll give you a swat on the behind."*

Threatening to hurt your child won't help him learn how to do what he's supposed to do. Instead, it will teach him that bigger, stronger people get to have their way.

Instead, use a chart. Say,

> *"Let's check the chart to see where you get to sit. Today's Monday,*
> *so that means you get to sit in the seat right behind Mommy!"*

Consider setting up a seating chart that alternates your child's seating position without compromising his safety. Relying on a prearranged seating chart helps prevent conflict and teaches your child about cooperation and sharing. It also helps him learn that cooperation makes everyone happy.

Chapter Twenty-five

"Please Talk to Your Daddy on the Phone." "No! I Don't Wanna Talk to Daddy on the Phone!"

This one hurts. You really want your four-year-old to talk to your ex, but she doesn't want to. It's important to put yourself in her shoes when she doesn't want to cooperate on the phone. She may be angry, worried, or upset that Mommy and Daddy live in separate houses. She may feel abandoned or unsure about what to say when her mother or father calls. It may be easier for her not to talk at all. Children come into the world able to feel empathy, and your job is to nurture and develop that ability. Over time your child will be able to put herself in your shoes and do a better job of cooperating.

Helpful Hints

✋ Make sure your child has the skills needed to participate in a phone conversation.

✋ Try to call your ex at a time when your child is most inclined to talk (after a nap, after a meal, in the morning, and so on).

✋ Talk about the importance of empathy, kindness, and caring so your child learns to think about how her behavior affects others.

✋ Encourage your child to talk about feelings, a practice that will enhance her natural empathy. While playing dollhouse with her, for example, have the dolls talk to each other about their feelings. See what your child "says" for the dolls.

Self-Talk

Don't tell yourself,
"I hate it when my child causes a problem between me and my ex."
Don't blame your child for conflicts between you and your ex. Your child's not wanting to talk to her other parent on the phone originates from the disruption of her life. Instead of blaming her, work to make her life as comfortable as possible in both homes.

Instead, tell yourself,

> *"I need to help my child understand how I might feel about her not wanting to talk to me on the phone."*

Focus on nurturing her empathy rather than squelching her rude behavior. This will help her learn to think about others' feelings when making decisions.

Don't tell yourself,

> *"What's her problem? I must be doing something wrong for her to act like this."*

Blaming yourself for your child's behavior suggests that you should have control over what she does. The truth is that she's an independent person who wants to make her own decisions.

Instead, tell yourself,

> *"It's not my fault that my child won't talk to her other parent on the phone."*

You can't control your child's behavior, but you can influence it. Increase her empathy and compassion by teaching her ways to relate to others with respect.

Don't tell yourself,

> *"I'm tired of fighting with her to talk to people on the phone. I don't care if she ever talks to anybody again."*

Giving up shows that you're not interested in working out a compromise and that quitting is okay. It also models a low tolerance for frustration and doesn't teach your child to empathize.

Instead, tell yourself,

> *"I care about her relationships and want her to appreciate how important it is to talk to each of her parents on the phone."*

Keep an objective response in mind when your child refuses to cooperate. The long-term goal is to help her develop kindness and empathy in her behavior toward others.

Talking to Your Child

Don't belittle. Don't say,

> ***"What's the matter with you?***
> ***Don't you know it's rude to refuse to talk to Daddy on the phone?"***

Don't suggest that there's something wrong with your child because she doesn't want to talk on the phone. She may be telling you that she needs help with her emotions, or she may not be ready to talk at that particular time. Your angry response won't encourage her to express her feelings.

Instead, empathize. Say,

> ***"I understand that you don't want to talk to Daddy right now.***
> ***Daddy very much wants to talk to you, and he feels a little***
> ***frustrated that you don't want to talk to him. But he***
> ***understands and he'll be available when you're ready."***

Encouraging your child to think about her other parent's feelings will help her reflect on how it would feel to be in her daddy's shoes. She'll also be able to think about how her decision affects others.

Don't make love conditional. Don't say,

> ***"Daddy won't love you anymore if you don't talk to him on the phone."***

Threatening loss of Daddy's (or Mommy's) love tells your child that she's only lovable when she's doing what her parents want. This is a dangerous and harmful message that teaches her that in order to be loved, she must always meet her parents' needs.

Instead, be understanding. Say,

> ***"Tell me what you're thinking about when you say you don't***
> ***want to talk to Daddy. Help me understand your decision."***

Asking for your child's thoughts opens a dialogue that can guide you toward a solution. It also models caring and empathy, two positive ways to interact with others.

Don't threaten. Don't say,

> *"If you don't talk to Daddy on the phone,*
> *you'll have to spend the day in your room."*

Threatening to isolate your child won't teach her to do what you've asked out of empathy for her other parent's feelings.

Instead, make a deal. Say,

> *"When you've talked to Daddy on the phone,*
> *then you may go outside and play."*

Grandma's Rule can provide the motivation your child needs to decide to talk to Daddy. It can also reinforce the importance of doing what needs to be done before doing what she wants.

Don't label. Don't say,

> *"I know you're shy, but you really need to talk to Daddy when he calls."*

Telling your child that she's shy establishes shyness as part of her personality, which may perpetuate the behavior.

Instead, offer support. Say,

> *"Daddy will be calling today. Let's practice some things to say to him,*
> *because he loves to talk to you on the phone."*

Suggest ways your child can feel comfortable doing something brave, such as talking to her father on the phone. Practicing the language ahead of time will make your child more comfortable with the experience.

SECTION V
PLAYING

No symphony orchestra ever played music
like a two-year-old girl laughing with a puppy.

—*Bern Williams*

Chapter Twenty-six

"Please Turn Off the TV."
"No! I Don't Wanna Turn Off the TV!"

TV's mesmerizing sounds and pictures can so entice a three-year-old that he can become addicted to watching this box of wonders. He has no concept of why this can become a dangerous pastime, so it's your responsibility to teach him. Provide him with other opportunities for entertainment, such as reading, games, and arts-and-crafts projects, and establish limits to govern his TV viewing.

Helpful Hints

🖐 Make rules about how much and what kind of TV is acceptable each day. The American Academy of Pediatrics recommends that parents limit TV time to no more than one to two hours of quality programming per day for children two years and older.[6]

🖐 Limit your own TV viewing so your child will follow your example.

🖐 Watch with your child to encourage him to be an active viewer. Ask him questions about the content and, if necessary, explain how advertisers try to manipulate his thoughts and feelings.

Self-Talk

Don't tell yourself,
"My child will become a fat, lazy bum if he sits in front of the TV all day."
Ouch! Labels hurt. Not only can they become self-fulfilling prophecies, they can also influence your attitude toward your child and damage his self-esteem.

Instead, tell yourself,
*"I understand my child's desire to watch TV,
but my job is to get him interested in other activities."*
Empathizing with your child's attraction to TV will help you address the problem with respect and patience.

Don't tell yourself,
"I don't know what to do when my child refuses to turn off the TV."
Telling yourself that you have no options won't help you solve the
problem. Such hopelessness will only make you feel overwhelmed
by the challenge.

Instead, tell yourself,
"I can cope with his resistance."
Giving yourself the confidence to cope reinforces your resolve to limit
his TV time when he resists. It's amazing how creative you can be
when you choose to have a positive attitude.

Don't tell yourself,
"I don't care how much TV my child watches. It can't hurt him."
Unfortunately, too much TV viewing can result in obesity, poor self-image,
decreased attention span, and aggressive behavior.[7] Don't ever give up!

Instead, tell yourself,
*"I need to enforce the rules about TV so my
child doesn't become addicted to it."*
Understanding the addictive nature of TV, demonstrating a willingness
to enforce limits, and providing your child with alternative activities
will help him avoid the problems associated with too much TV viewing.

Talking to Your Child

Don't belittle. Don't say,
*"What's the matter with you? I told you to turn off the TV.
Are you deaf?"*
If you know your child doesn't have a hearing problem and is just
ignoring you, don't ask such a belittling question. Stick to the goal of
teaching him to follow your directions.

Instead, offer solutions. Say,
*"I understand that you don't want to turn off the TV, but you've used
up your TV time for the day. Let's think of other fun things you can do."*
Your empathy and understanding, as well as your reminder of the rule,
will help your child learn that it's important to follow the rules. Letting
him know that you're sensitive to his needs and desires will strengthen
your relationship and encourage his cooperation.

Don't threaten. Don't say,

> *"If you don't get off your rear end and turn off the TV,*
> *you'll be sorry, mister."*

Threatening to punish your child will either encourage him to avoid you or will entice him to test your threat by refusing to cooperate.

Instead, make a deal. Say,

> *"When you turn off the TV, then you may watch*
> *one of your favorite programs later. If you don't turn it off now,*
> *then TV time is over for the day."*

Grandma's Rule, which encourages children to earn their privileges, will help your child learn to delay gratification and do what he needs to do before getting to do what he wants to do.

Don't tattle. Don't say,

> *"When your father gets home, I'm going to tell him*
> *you wouldn't turn off the TV when I told you to."*

Tattling to the other parent tells your child that you're not able to enforce the rules, which damages your credibility. Using fear of the other parent's anger will also diminish your child's ability to empathize.

Instead, remind him about the rule. Say,

> *"When this program is over, the rule says TV time is over."*

Reminding your child of the rule gives him time to prepare for the end of the activity. This teaches him that you and he can work together to meet both of your agendas.

Chapter Twenty-seven

"Please Play by Yourself for a While."
"No! I Don't Wanna Play by Myself!"

Here's the paradox of your preschooler's development: While she would rather be with you than do anything else, she's also trying to separate from you and establish her own identity. Reassuring her and supporting her independence will pay off as she learns to navigate the world just like her hero—you!

Helpful Hints

🖐 Understand your child's developmental need to frequently "tag up" to you as "home base," just to know you're there. (See Milestones of Development on pages 227–229.)

🖐 Let your child play near you while you're busy with other things, such as talking on the phone, so she can see you and hear you while she's playing independently.

🖐 Encourage your child's independent play by providing interactive toys that require her manipulation.

🖐 Schedule play time with your child each day so she'll know she'll have that time exclusively with you.

🖐 Make sure your child's play area is safe, comfortable, and inviting.

Self-Talk

Don't tell yourself,
"Why can't she see that I'm too busy to play with her?"
Your child has no understanding of your other responsibilities and the time they require. All she's thinking is, "I want Mommy." Change your exasperated tone into a patient one by empathizing with your child's desire to be with you.

Instead, tell yourself,

*"I understand my child's desire to be near
me after being away from me all day."*

Empathizing with your child's need to reconnect helps you stay in touch
with your own need to stay connected. Put your other duties aside for
a few minutes, or figure out ways to let your child help with chores.

Don't tell yourself,

*"I feel guilty when I get home and the dishes
are piled up and I can't play with my child."*

Guilt results from telling yourself that you've done something wrong.
It's a harmful response because it may lead you to overcompensate and
spoil your child to win her love.

Instead, tell yourself,

"I can handle sending her to play by herself, even if she cries."

Sometimes circumstances require you to put other things ahead of your
child. Having the strength to enforce your boundaries will help you avoid
feeling guilt and anger. Remember, only *you* can make you feel guilty.

Don't tell yourself,

"Other parents can get their children to play by themselves. Why can't I?"

Comparing yourself to other parents is distracting and destructive.
Telling yourself that you're not a good parent will harm your ability
to solve the problem. Your relationship with your child is unique,
and you need to address it on its own terms.

Instead, tell yourself,

*"My child has a mind of her own,
and her resistance doesn't mean I'm a bad parent."*

Understand that children can be fiercely independent, regardless of
how they're parented. When your agendas don't match, you and your
child need to learn to compromise and work together as a team.

Talking to Your Child

Don't use guilt. Don't say,

"Shut up about wanting somebody to play with!
How many times do I have to tell you I'm too busy?"

The "how many times" guilt trip will only make your child feel bad; it won't show her how to entertain herself. In addition, modeling abusive language will only teach your child to use it, too.

Instead, make a deal. Say,

"I know you want me to play with you, but I need to talk on the
phone right now. I'll set the timer for ten minutes. When you play by
yourself until the timer rings, then we can play a game together."

Use a timer to help your child learn to play on her own. If necessary, practice the timer game when it's not urgently needed to make sure your child understands how it works.

Don't give in. Don't say,

"Okay, stop whining. I'll quit folding laundry and play with you.
I don't care if we don't have any clean clothes."

Giving in to your child's whining only encourages her to continue using this strategy to get what she wants.

Instead, make a deal. Say,

"When you play by yourself until I finish putting away the laundry,
we can play dollhouse until it's time for dinner."

Grandma's Rule will help your child learn to compromise and delay gratification in order to get what she wants—time with you.

Don't threaten. Don't say,

"If you don't stop whining about having to play by yourself,
I'm going to make you stay in your room all day.
Then maybe you'll learn to entertain yourself."

Don't punish your child for not being able to entertain herself. It won't teach her how to accomplish that goal, and it will discourage her from telling you what she wants appropriately.

Instead, offer choices. Say,

"You may stay here and play until I've finished the dishes, or you may play in your room until I'm available. You decide."

Instead of punishing your child for trying to get your attention, give her the choice of staying near you while you finish your chores. This win-win solution teaches her that compromising can help her meet her agenda.

Don't use anger. Don't say,

"I'm sick and tired of your constant whining for attention. Do you think all I have to do is play with you?"

Don't use anger to try to motivate your child's independence. Doing so will erode her empathy and teach her that wanting to be with you isn't important to you—a hurtful, abusive message.

Instead, be grateful. Say,

"I'm so glad you want to play with me. I want to play with you, too. When I've finished my work and you've finished your play, we can play together."

Being grateful for your child's desire to be with you teaches her that she's a valued person in your life. In addition, providing a future payoff of your time and attention can reinforce her ability to play by herself.

Chapter Twenty-eight

"Please Stop Playing Your Video Game." "No! I Don't Wanna Stop Playing My Video Game!"

If you love playing on the computer, chances are your little one does, too. While spending hours on the computer may be essential to your job (or may be one of your favorite pastimes), your five-year-old's jobs are spending time playing with other children, exercising his developing body, and stimulating his mind with the sights and sounds of the real world. He may not immediately value the healthy habits you're trying to teach, but limiting the time he spends playing electronic games and other sedentary activities will help prevent childhood obesity and its various side effects: high blood pressure, type II diabetes, and heart disease.[8]

Helpful Hints

✋ Set a timer to signal when a video game or computer needs to be turned off.

✋ Provide a variety of stimulating materials (picture books, dress-up clothes, markers, paper, crayons, coloring books, arts-and-crafts supplies, and so on) to encourage your child's imagination and creativity.

✋ Screen the content of all video and computer games before letting your child use them. Ensure that they depict healthy relationships, model nonviolent behaviors, and send positive messages.

✋ Limit your use of video and computer games while your preschooler is nearby.

Self-Talk

Don't tell yourself,

"Why doesn't he do what I tell him to do? He never listens to me!"

Don't take your child's refusal to stop playing video games personally. He's not rejecting you; he simply wants to continue his fun.

Instead, tell yourself,

> *"I can remain calm when he refuses my request."*

Managing your emotions will model the behavior you want your child to imitate as he learns to cope with frustration. In addition, not taking the situation personally will help you react to his behavior with patience and support.

Don't tell yourself,

> *"He's such a stubborn child. I don't know what to do with him."*

Labeling your child as stubborn creates a self-fulfilling prophecy that will encourage him to live *down* to your expectations.

Instead, tell yourself,

> *"My job is to understand my child's strengths and interests and direct them in positive ways."*

Remember that your first priority is to teach your child to become self-disciplined. Redirect his attention when he begins to spend too much time on any one activity.

Don't tell yourself,

> *"I don't care if he spends all his time playing on the computer. At least he's out of my hair, and I know where he is."*

Your job is to guide your child toward constructive activities that will nurture his development. Don't be discouraged when he doesn't want to follow your directions.

Instead, tell yourself,

> *"I like interacting with my child and don't want him to view the computer as his only friend."*

Daily interactions with you and others will lead your child to develop good social skills. Keep this in mind when he begs for more computer time.

Talking to Your Child

Don't use vague threats. Don't say,

"I told you to stop playing your video game, and I meant it. If I have to come in there and tell you one more time, you'll be sorry."

Vague threats of "one more time" only encourage your child to push your limits rather than follow the rule. When that happens, you're forced to follow through with some kind of punishment, or risk losing your credibility. Don't force yourself into a corner with a lose-lose strategy.

Instead, use the timer. Say,

"When the timer rings, it's time to put away your game and find something else to do."

Set limits and use the timer to signal when the limit has been reached. Respecting limits will become a healthy habit your child can use in other situations as he gets older.

Don't shame. Don't say,

"Do you want to become a fat, lazy kid? You will if you don't stop playing that computer game and don't get any exercise."

Don't tell your child that he'll become fat and lazy in the future. It's not a concept he'll be able to grasp now, so it's ineffective in motivating him to follow the rule. It can, however, become a self-fulfilling prophecy if you say it repeatedly.

Instead, praise cooperative behavior. Say,

"Thank you for putting away your video game when I asked you to."

Praising your child's cooperation provides him with what he wants most: your attention and compliments.

Don't compare. Don't say,

"Why can't you mind me when I tell you to do something? You're just like your father. He never listens to me either."

Telling your child that he's behaving like another family member puts both of them in a negative light, which doesn't teach your child how to cooperate.

Instead, make a deal. Say,

> *"When you stop playing when the timer rings,*
> *then you'll get to play again later."*

Grandma's Rule teaches your child that when he does what he has to do, then he gets to do what he wants to do. This enables both of your agendas to be met.

Don't threaten. Don't say,

> *"If you don't stop playing now, I'll have to spank you."*

Threatening your child with physical pain may achieve short-term results, but it won't teach him the long-term benefit of cooperating. Instead, it will drive the behavior underground. He'll continue to play as long as he thinks he can get away with it. He won't learn the self-discipline he needs to limit the activity on his own.

Instead, use time-out. Say,

> *"I'm sorry you didn't stop when your time was up.*
> *Now the game will have to go into time-out for the rest of the day."*

Saying you're sorry models empathy for your child and lets him know you understand that stopping his fun was hard for him. Removing the game for a period of time teaches him that his lack of cooperation will result in negative consequences.

Chapter Twenty-nine

"Please Play Quietly While the Baby's Sleeping." "No! I Don't Wanna Play Quietly!"

This is another perfect opportunity to elicit your child's innate capacity for empathy. Tell her you understand that it's hard for her to play quietly when she's having so much fun, but gently explain that being kind to someone else will make her feel good, too. Help her learn that kindness is magical: The more you give it away, the more you get it back.

Helpful Hints

🖐 Make rules about playing quietly during the baby's nap. Give your child advance notice that in five minutes, for example, you're going to put the baby down. Then quiet time will begin.

🖐 Use a baby monitor so you can hear what's going on in the baby's room while you and your toddler are playing in another room. This way you won't have to constantly shush your toddler to listen for the baby.

🖐 Help your child understand exactly what you mean when you ask her to be quiet. She may think she's not allowed to speak or move! Demonstrate the kind of voice you want her to use, and encourage her to avoid making sudden loud noises.

🖐 Toddlers are naturally noisy, so be prepared to put up with an occasional *thump*, *squeal*, or *bang*. Luckily, babies are designed to endure a certain amount of noise while sleeping.

Self-Talk

Don't tell yourself,

"What's the matter with her? Doesn't she care about the baby? How can she not get it?"

Don't label your child as uncaring because she doesn't always remember the quiet rule. Babies change the family dynamic, and adjusting to this change takes time.

Instead, tell yourself,

> *"My job is to teach my child to understand the*
> *need to be quiet while the baby's sleeping."*

Reframe the situation in terms of teaching your child to empathize. This will help you work together to care for the new arrival. Praise her cooperation whenever possible, to reinforce the desired behavior.

Don't tell yourself,

> *"I can't put up with the noise any longer.*
> *I need some quiet and so does the baby."*

Telling yourself you can't cope with something hinders your ability to cope.

Instead, tell yourself,

> *"I don't like my daughter's noise, but I can deal with it."*

Tell yourself that you'd like your child to follow the quiet rule, but it won't be the end of the world if she occasionally forgets. Letting her make mistakes will demonstrate your empathy, tolerance, acceptance, and unconditional love.

Don't tell yourself,

> *"I'll make her be quiet if it's the last thing I do."*

When you make your child's cooperation a matter of life or death, you exaggerate the problem and make it unsolvable. Her noise is beyond your control, but your reaction is not.

Instead, tell yourself,

> *"I can choose to be understanding when my child forgets the quiet rule."*

Choosing a "no big deal" response to your older child's mistake will prevent the situation from escalating into a full-blown power struggle. Remember that all events are neutral; we label them as negative or positive.

Talking to Your Child

Don't belittle. Don't say,

> *"What's wrong with you? I told you to be quiet!"*

There's nothing wrong with your child. She's just being a normal preschooler who wants to talk, sing, dance, and make her presence known. Your job is to teach her to put herself in another person's shoes, and to model that behavior yourself.

Instead, play the quiet game. Whisper,

"It's quiet time now. Let's see how quiet we can be. Shhhh. Hear the clock tick? Isn't it nice and peaceful when it's quiet? When the baby wakes up, quiet time will be over. Let's enjoy it as long as we can."

Point out the value of quiet time to help your child learn to enjoy it. Your positive attitude will encourage her to follow your directions as you play the game.

Don't use anger. Don't say,

"Why can't you be quiet like I asked you? You're making me mad!"

Avoid "why" questions that automatically make your child defensive, thereby discouraging her from wanting to do what you ask. Attacking her for simply wanting to have fun will alienate her, not encourage her to cooperate.

Instead, use the timer. Say,

"It's going to be time for the baby's nap in five minutes. When the timer rings, quiet time starts. Let's get ready."

Letting your child anticipate what's going to happen gives her time to shift into quiet mode. Using the timer to control the situation helps prevent conflict and makes quiet time easier to handle.

Don't bribe. Don't say,

"If you can stay quiet while the baby's sleeping, I'll give you some ice cream when he wakes up."

Bribing your child with food makes her think she can charge you a price for cooperating. This doesn't teach her to follow directions so she feels good about helping the baby sleep.

Instead, praise cooperative behavior. Say,

"You're playing so quietly. Thank you so much for following the quiet rule and helping the baby take a good nap. Babies really need their sleep."

Praise your child's quiet play, linking it to her natural empathy. Your praise will reinforce her willingness to cooperate and will expand her ability to empathize.

Chapter Thirty

"Please Share."
"No! I Don't Wanna Share!"

One of the most remarkable things about children is how they develop according to their own timetable. Some children understand the concept of sharing at age two, while others develop the skill at age four or five. Make it your goal to encourage sharing in children of all ages, and realize that it's a skill that every child needs to have continually reinforced. Even adults need to be reminded now and again!

Helpful Hints

✋ Make rules about sharing. For example, "When you put a toy on the floor, anyone may play with it. When you have it in your hand, you may keep it."

✋ Point out examples of sharing so your child can learn how it works: for example, when you give him part of your sandwich, or when you let him wear your shoes to play dress-up.

✋ Let your child put away a few favorite toys before friends come over.

✋ Start your own family outreach program by sharing unused toys and clothing with those who are less fortunate.

Self-Talk

Don't tell yourself,
"If he can't share his toys, I won't get him any more."
Refusing to buy toys won't teach your child to share. Instead, it will establish an unhealthy, rigid, punishing mentality. Look for ways to compromise instead of making rules that deny your child any hope of getting his way.

Instead, tell yourself,
"I understand that it's difficult for my child to give up his precious possessions, even for a little while."
He needs to know that you understand and sympathize with his reluctance to share.

Don't tell yourself,

> **"It's okay that he doesn't want to share.**
> **Other children would just break his toys anyway."**

Don't excuse your child's selfishness by making him the victim of others' destructive behavior. Doing so won't teach him to work and play well with others.

Instead, tell yourself,

> **"It's important for me to point out how others feel when he doesn't share."**

Your goal is to help your child learn to think about others' feelings as well as his own.

Don't tell yourself,

> **"My child is a selfish brat who won't share."**

Labeling not only blames your child for developmentally appropriate behavior, it can become a self-fulfilling prophecy. If you treat him like he's a brat, he's likely to act like one.

Instead, tell yourself,

> **"My child is simply doing what kids his age do."**

Recognizing the egocentric nature of preschool children helps you understand that it's normal for them not to want to share. This thinking helps you avoid getting upset over your child's behavior.

Talking to Your Child

Don't use putdowns. Don't say,

> **"You're such a selfish child. Nobody will want to play with you."**

Predicting your child's social isolation won't teach him to share, but it may become a self-fulfilling prophecy.

Instead, remind him about the rule. Say,

> **"Remember, when your friend has a toy, you have to**
> **wait until he puts it down before you can play with it."**

Reminding your child about the rule helps him remember it and connect it to the immediate situation. Focusing on what you want him to learn is much more effective than focusing on the negative behavior.

Don't ask unanswerable questions. Don't say,
> *"Why can't you share your toys?"*

Asking your child to explain why he can't share is like asking a baby to explain why he can't crawl.

Instead, offer support. Say,
> *"I know it's hard to share sometimes. I'll stay with you and your friend while you play, so I can help you share with each other."*

How nice to have a coach to teach you a difficult skill! Taking this approach puts you and your child on the same team. Supervising his play also gives you the opportunity to praise sharing and to stop squabbling before it escalates.

Don't threaten. Don't say,
> *"If you don't share your toys, I'll just throw them in the trash. That'll teach you."*

Idle threats won't teach your child to share. He may take your threat to heart and share for the moment, but he'll do so only to avoid losing the toys, not because he cares about others' feelings.

Instead, use time-out. Say,
> *"I'm sorry that toy is causing problems between the two of you. It will have to go into time-out for a while."*

Temporarily removing a "troublemaking" toy will reduce conflict without shaming either child. It will also give you a chance to remind them about the rule.

Don't beg. Don't say,
> *"Won't you please share? Do it for Mommy, please!"*

Begging teaches your child to share only to avoid losing your love and approval, not because he wants to work and play well with others.

Instead, use a timer. Say,
> *"I'll set the timer. When it rings, it'll be time to give the toy to your brother so he can play with it until the timer rings again. Isn't that a nice way to share?"*

Using a timer to enforce the sharing rule puts the timer in control, not you. This helps you focus on encouraging your child to follow the rule.

Chapter Thirty-one

"Please Turn Down the Music."
"No! I Don't Wanna Turn Down the Music!"

Sometimes playing music at high volume is just what a five-year-old (or an adult!) needs. However, being considerate of those around you is a necessary part of living together and getting along. When your child wants to crank up the volume, turn the potential problem into a teachable moment while modeling respect for her burgeoning interest in music.

Helpful Hints

❧ Make a rule about appropriate volume levels. Mark the volume control with a piece of tape, or remind your child of the volume number that should not be exceeded (for digital volume controls).

❧ Don't complain about turning the music down when somebody asks you to do so.

❧ Model respect for others by asking them if the music is too loud or not loud enough.

❧ Have your child's hearing checked to make sure a hearing problem isn't causing her desire for high volume.

❧ Consider having your child use headphones if her musical tastes and volume needs aren't compatible with other family members. Make sure her CD or tape player doesn't have unsafe volume levels that would threaten her hearing.

Self-Talk

Don't tell yourself,

"My child will be deaf before she's a teenager if she keeps the volume so high."

Focusing on the worst-case scenario can lead you to behave irrationally as you strive to correct the problem. Instead, take reasonable, positive steps to teach your child to control the volume.

Instead, tell yourself,

"I can handle the noise without getting stressed-out."
Your parents probably had to teach you to control the volume, so keep in mind how their words made you feel as you talk lovingly to your child about the problem.

Don't tell yourself,

"My child is so inconsiderate that I'm having trouble tolerating her behavior."
Labeling your child as inconsiderate makes her desire to keep the volume up a permanent problem. It also teaches her that your love is conditional—that it's only there when she does what you want.

Instead, tell yourself,

"My goal is teaching my child to be considerate of others."
Keeping the larger goal in mind lets you focus on helping your child use her natural empathy to think about others' needs.

Don't tell yourself,

"I guess I'll let her play the volume as loudly as she wants. I'm tired of fighting with her about it."
Giving in to your child's demand to play music loudly shows her how to give up when faced with opposition. In addition, allowing her to play music as loud as she wants as long as she wants may jeopardize her hearing.

Instead, tell yourself,

"Giving up shirks my responsibility to teach my child to cooperate with others."
Even though you may be tired and stressed-out, it's important to put your parenting responsibility first. Teaching your child cooperation can benefit her for a lifetime.

Talking to Your Child

Don't threaten. Don't say,

"If you don't turn that down, I'm going to come in there and smack you."
Never threaten your child with physical violence to get her to follow the rules. Doing so may work in the short term, but it won't help her learn the lesson you want to teach: being considerate of others' feelings.

Instead, state the problem. Say,

"I know you like the volume loud, but it hurts my ears.
You need to turn it down."

Telling your child about the impact her loud volume has on you encourages her to use her natural empathy. Instead of screaming at her to do what you want, explain the reasoning behind your request. Your child will feel important because you respect her enough to tell her the truth.

Don't punish. Don't say,

"I'm sick and tired of that loud music.
Give me that CD player so I can throw it away!"

Don't tell your child that you're going to destroy her CD player to get her to cooperate. A drastic, destructive "solution" may stop the noise, but it won't help her learn the importance of cooperation. In fact, it suggests that if she misbehaves, she can be thrown out, too.

Instead, use time-out. Say,

"I'm sorry you didn't remember to keep the volume down.
Now the CD player will have to go into time-out until tomorrow."

Enforcing the volume rule tells your child she must keep the volume down to keep her CD player on. Putting the machine in time-out is an effective strategy because the volume gets turned down (to "off") and your child learns the importance of following the rules.

Don't bribe. Don't say,

"If you keep the volume down, I'll buy you some new CDs."

Bribing your child with more music to get her to keep the volume down teaches her that she should be rewarded for doing what you ask.

Instead, make a deal. Say,

"When you keep the volume where we marked it,
you may use your CD player."

Grandma's Rule tells your child that when she follows the rules, she gets to do what she wants to do.

SECTION VI
CLEANUP ROUTINES

Boredom arises from routine.
Joy, wonder, and rapture arise from surprise.
—*Leo Buscaglia*

Chapter Thirty-two

"Please Clean Up Your Toys."
"No! I Don't Wanna Clean Up!"

When your four-year-old ignores your request to clean up his toys, he's telling you that his agenda doesn't match yours. He wants to continue playing and making a mess, while you want to restore order to the ransacked area. Two- and three-year-olds often need help knowing where to start cleaning up, but four- and five-year-olds can better grasp the concept and follow it through to completion—if they've been practicing.

Helpful Hints

✋ Encourage your child's cleanup habit by establishing a simple rule: Before getting out another toy, you must put away the one you're playing with.

✋ Make it easy for your child to pick up his things so he'll be more inclined to follow the rule. For example, set up low-level shelves and bins for easy storage.

✋ Include your child in family cleanup routines so he can learn by watching and doing.

✋ Consider limiting the number of toys available to your child by dividing his toys into four groups and putting away all but one group. At the end of the week, put away that group and get another one out for the next week.

Self-Talk

Don't tell yourself,

"What's the matter with him?
Why can't this messy child be like his neat sister?"

Some children are naturally better at organization and cleanliness. Tidiness isn't a priority for others, but they can learn to value it with your encouragement and support. Approach your children individually, and avoid comparing them to each other. Doing so only encourages sibling rivalry and jealousy.

Instead, tell yourself,

> *"Just because my older child is a neatnik*
> *doesn't mean my younger one must be."*

Understanding that children are different will discourage you from expecting one to behave like the other.

Don't tell yourself,

> *"My child is messy just like his father."*

Don't label your child or blame his messiness on his other parent. Doing so dooms him to a life of clutter, confirms that you're helpless to teach him new behavior, and damages his perception of his other parent.

Instead, tell yourself,

> *"I know getting my child to clean up is a hassle,*
> *but I always feel better when things are tidy and organized."*

Focus on the positive outcome, not on your child's messiness or lack of cooperation. This will keep you and your child working toward the goal.

Don't tell yourself,

> *"My child won't listen to me when I tell him to clean up."*

Consider the possibility that listening may not be the problem. Instead, your child may not know where to begin or may see the task as overwhelming. Assess his skill level by asking him to show you how to put blocks away, for example.

Instead, tell yourself,

> *"A little effort now can establish a lifelong habit."*

Working with your child, praising his efforts, and celebrating the outcome will focus positive attention on teamwork and cooperation. Look past the short-term challenge to the long-term goal of teaching him good cleanup habits.

Talking to Your Child

Don't nag. Don't say,

> *"How many times do I have to tell you to pick up your clothes?"*

No one wants to be around a nag. Nagging only teaches your child to tune you out and to use nagging to motivate others. It doesn't teach him to value neatness or show him how to accomplish it.

Instead, remind him about the rule. Say,

> **"Remember, the rule says you can get out another toy when you've put away the one you're finished with."**

Gently reminding your child of the rule teaches him much more than cooperation: It teaches him that organization and order are important. In addition, when you set rules to encourage your child to cooperate, you give him practice in how the world works. Following rules is common: obeying traffic lights, paying for what you buy, and so on. It's never too early to begin practicing.

Don't threaten. Don't say,

> **"If you don't put away your toys, I'll just throw them in the trash."**

Telling your child that you'll throw away his toys if he doesn't comply means you'll have to follow through if he calls your bluff—a costly consequence for both of you. Plus, it won't teach him how to pick up after himself.

Instead, make it a game. Say,

> **"Let's set the timer and see if we can finish cleaning up before it rings."**

Using a timer puts it—not you—in control. Working together reinforces the value of teamwork and gives you the opportunity to praise your child's effort.

Don't label. Don't say,

> **"No wonder you can't pick up after yourself.
> You're a slob just like your mother."**

Avoid hurtful words. They're never worth the pain they cause, and they only serve to create more conflict. In addition, labeling your child a slob may become a self-fulfilling prophecy.

Instead, empathize. Say,

> **"I know it's hard to clean up when you want to keep playing.
> I understand how you feel."**

If you're a little "cleaning challenged" yourself, admitting this flaw to your child will show empathy for his situation and will help you work together to tackle the job.

Don't bribe. Don't say,

> *"If you clean up, I'll buy you some more toys."*

Bribing your child doesn't teach him the skill you want him to learn, and it doesn't help him develop a healthy attitude toward organization and tidiness. Instead, it teaches him that his cooperation is for sale, and he can hold out for the highest price.

Instead, make a deal. Say,

> *"When we get all your toys picked up and put away, then we can play a game together."*

Use Grandma's Rule to teach your child that meeting your agenda helps him meet his agenda.

Chapter Thirty-three

"Please Get Out of the Bathtub."
"No! I Don't Wanna Get Out of the Tub!"

Be careful what you wish for...you might get it! Helping your three-year-old have fun in the tub is an important step in encouraging her to get *in* the tub. However, after you've made tub time so much fun, it's natural for her not to want to get out. Prepare a comfy exit by providing lots of towels and hugs for warmth and security.

Helpful Hints

✋ Set limits for tub time, and use a timer to enforce the limits.

✋ Start the bathtub routine early to avoid having to rush your child's fun.

✋ *Never* leave toddlers and preschoolers alone in the bathtub, even for a few seconds.

✋ Set your water heater at 120°F (or lower) to prevent the bath water from scalding your child.

Self-Talk

Don't tell yourself,
> *"I hate this nightly battle over getting out of the tub."*

Resenting your child for "putting you in this situation" will only increase your anxiety and discourage her cooperation.

Instead, tell yourself,
> *"I can cope with my child's refusal to get out of the tub.*
> *She's having so much fun, I can hardly blame her!"*

Putting a positive spin on the situation will help keep your tone friendly and your words kind.

Don't tell yourself,

"I can't go through the bathtub battle tonight. I just don't have the energy."

Don't go here! This sets up the expectation that bath time will be stressful and prevents you from mustering the strength and patience to deal with it. If you anticipate a battle, you'll probably get one.

Instead, tell yourself,

"I understand her desire to have fun splashing in the water."

Empathizing with your child's needs and desires allows you to maintain a good relationship with her, and your positive attitude encourages her cooperation.

Don't tell yourself,

"I have things I need to do.
I can't spend time watching her play in the tub."

Putting your agenda ahead of your child's will prevent you from being "in the moment" with her. She'll likely resist following your directions in order to get your attention.

Instead, tell yourself,

"My job is to teach her to cooperate,
and compromising will help her learn to do that."

Set a timer for a few minutes if she's not quite ready to stop her fun, but tell her that when the timer rings, it'll be time to get out. Keeping her agenda in mind helps everyone's needs get met.

Talking to Your Child

Don't threaten. Don't say,

"Get out of the tub NOW before I smack you on your bare bottom."

Don't threaten to hurt your child! Doing so might get immediate results, but the pain—emotional and physical—is too high a price to pay.

Instead, use a timer. Say,

"When the timer rings, it will be time to get out
and dry off so we can have a story before bed."

Use a timer to manage the situation, and provide an incentive (such as a story) to motivate your child's cooperation. This allows her to look beyond her desire to stay in the tub.

Don't minimize your child's feelings. Don't say,

"I have better things to do, so you need to get out of the tub now."

Telling your child that you have more important things to do will make her feel unwanted and unworthy of your attention. Instead of cooperating, she'll do everything she can to resist your request so she can finally get your attention.

Instead, remind her about the rule. Say,

"What's the rule about staying in the tub?"

Referring to the rule helps your child develop the self-discipline she'll need throughout her lifetime. It also puts you in a supportive rather than controlling role.

Don't get angry. Don't say,

"I'm getting angry, so you'd better get out of the tub before I lose my temper."

Getting angry won't teach your child to cooperate, and it won't model the self-control you want her to develop. It will do just the opposite: teach her to throw a tantrum in order to get her way.

Instead, give consequences. Say,

"I'm sorry you spent too much time in the tub. Now we don't have time for your snack or story."

Allow your child to suffer the consequences of failing to meet her goals. Doing so teaches her that her behavior has consequences—both positive and negative. It also gives her experience in coping with life's little disappointments.

Don't bribe. Don't say,

"If you get out of the tub now, I'll give you some candy."

Bribing your child with candy will leave a bad taste in your mouth! It will make that treat very important to her and will teach her that she can put a price on her cooperation.

Instead, make a deal. Say,

"When you've gotten out of the tub and are dry and in your pajamas, we can read a story before you go to bed."

Grandma's Rule helps your child develop self-control and the ability to delay gratification. These skills will help her cope with the necessary and sometimes unpleasant tasks of life.

Chapter Thirty-four

"Please Brush Your Teeth."
"No! I Don't Wanna Brush My Teeth!"

Perhaps you dreaded brushing your teeth when you were young—and maybe you still do! If your child resists brushing his teeth, look beyond the color of his toothbrush or the taste of his toothpaste to the root of the problem: his need to control his world. Give him a sense of control (and help him learn that maintaining healthy teeth and gums can be fun) by letting him select his own dental products.

Helpful Hints

✋ Whenever possible, brush your teeth with your child so he can see how it's done and be motivated to do the same.

✋ Find a kid-friendly dentist who supports your efforts to encourage good dental hygiene. If possible, interview a couple of dentists to learn how they work with young children.

Self-Talk

Don't tell yourself,
"My child makes me so mad when he doesn't want to do what's good for him."
Don't tell yourself that your child has power over your feelings. This diminishes your self-control and puts the responsibility on him instead of you.

Instead, tell yourself,
"I'm not going to get upset over his resistance. My getting angry won't help him learn to cooperate."
Affirming your desire to stay calm in the face of adversity will provide a good model for your child and will give you the energy and creativity you need to solve the problem. This situation begs for humor and fun; both are hard to come by when you're upset. A little humor goes a long way toward keeping your emotions positive while getting your child to cooperate.

Don't tell yourself,

"Why can't he just cooperate? He's so stubborn."

Drop the labels! When you call your child stubborn, his resistance becomes a part of him rather than a passing problem. Remember your parenting mantra: "This too shall pass."

Instead, tell yourself,

"I'm not going to get into a battle with my child over brushing his teeth. It'll only make it harder for both of us."

Fighting over small issues will turn your household into a battleground where nobody wins. Consider tooth brushing an everyday habit, like washing hands before dinner or brushing hair before school. Your child will learn to do it as a normal part of his day.

Don't tell yourself,

"His teeth can just rot for all I care. I can't stand to fight with him every day."

Choosing to run away from the problem is bad for your child's health and doesn't teach him to cooperate. Focus on the goal, not on his rebellion.

Instead, tell yourself,

"I have to keep the goal in mind."

Prioritizing the long-term goal of teaching good dental hygiene helps you keep the small battles in perspective. Staying positive will help your child do the same. His resistance can't wear down your commitment to being a teaching parent. Only you can make that decision.

Talking to Your Child

Don't get angry. Don't say,

"I'm sick and tired of your not wanting to brush your teeth. Now get in there and don't come out till you've finished."

Demanding cooperation sets up battle lines with your child; it doesn't show him how to be more cooperative. Forcing the issue will only result in greater resistance. Make peace, not war!

Instead, give choices. Say,

"I understand that you don't like to brush your teeth, but it's very important to keep them clean and healthy. Do you want me to help you brush, or do you want to do it yourself?"

Taking a helpful, supportive approach can soften your child's resistance. Working together can meet his agenda (having some control) and yours (getting his teeth brushed).

Don't use putdowns. Don't say,

"You're so pigheaded. I don't know what I'm going to do with you."

Labeling your child equates his behavior with who he is, contributing to a negative self-image. Make sure to separate your child from his behavior, so he understands that he may behave in undesirable ways at times, but that he can change his behavior. Make sure your child knows that he's always lovable and wonderful even when his behavior is not.

Instead, invite feedback. Say,

"Tell me what you don't like about brushing. I'd like to help if I can."

Asking your child for his opinion validates him as a person and gives you information that may solve the problem.

Don't bribe. Don't say,

"If you brush your teeth, I'll let you have some soda pop."

Offering your child a reward for doing what you ask sends him the message that cooperation is all about the reward, not about teamwork. Besides, giving a sugary snack or drink defeats the purpose of brushing.

Instead, make a deal. Say,

"When your teeth are clean, then we can read some bedtime stories."

Grandma's Rule teaches your child that in order to do what he wants, he must first accomplish the required task. This important lesson also teaches him the goal of cooperation: a win-win result.

Chapter Thirty-five

"It's Time to Get Your Hair Cut."
"No! I Don't Wanna Get My Hair Cut!"

Those sharp scissors. That big, scary chair. That cold metal touching your child's skin. Getting a haircut can be a nightmare for an inexperienced two-year-old. When you put yourself in your child's shoes, you can understand why she's protesting the trip to the hair salon. Try to find the right person for the job (barber, stylist, friend, or yourself) to help turn her fear into fun.

Helpful Hints

✋ Play hairstylist at home to give your child some practice in getting her hair cut.

✋ Talk about the fun parts of getting a haircut, such as the buzzing razor tickling her neck or how good it feels to have her scalp massaged.

✋ Make sure the person cutting your child's hair is experienced, patient, and nurturing.

✋ Stay by your child's side during the haircut to help her feel safe.

Self-Talk

Don't tell yourself,
"What's the matter with my child?
Why can't she just sit quietly and get her hair cut?"
Don't assume something is wrong with your child when she fears things. It's perfectly normal for her to worry about what a scissors-wielding stranger might do to her.

Instead, tell yourself,
"My child's resistance is understandable.
My job is to help her overcome her fear."
Use empathy to remind yourself how your child feels, but keep the goal in mind to help you get the job done.

Don't tell yourself,
"Why is my child doing this to me? I wish she'd just cooperate for a change."
Avoid taking your child's resistance personally. Doing so makes you a victim, keeps you from focusing on her needs, and prevents you from finding creative ways to help her overcome her fear.

Instead, tell yourself,
"I can handle my child's fear of getting a haircut."
This affirmation helps you cope with the challenge and work out a solution. You *can* teach her to cooperate, but first you have to tell yourself you can.

Don't tell yourself,
"What will the people in the salon think about me if I have to fight my child to get her hair cut?"
Worrying about what others think will make you feel anxious and will distract you from helping your child. Don't let others' opinions (real or imagined) influence your behavior toward your child.

Instead, tell yourself,
"I don't need to feel embarrassed when my child fights getting her hair cut."
Refusing to feel embarrassed will help you focus on your child's needs.

Don't tell yourself,
"I give up. I don't care if she gets her hair cut."
Don't give up! Your job is to help your child learn ways to overcome her fears. This task may take several visits to the barbershop or hair salon, so be patient.

Instead, tell yourself,
"As I learn how to encourage my child's cooperation, I'm improving my leadership skills."
Being a good leader is an excellent way to frame your role as a parent. Model good leadership by supporting your child even though she isn't following your directions. Your patience, love, and positive attitude will help her learn to cooperate at haircut time.

Talking to Your Child

Don't demand. Don't say,

> *"What do you mean you don't want a haircut?*
> *Now just shut up and get in the chair!"*

Your lack of empathy for your child's feelings will diminish her ability to identify her emotions and deal with them. In addition, it will make her lose respect for you, which will increase her desire to rebel.

Instead, invite feedback. Say,

> *"Tell me how you feel inside when your hair is getting cut."*

Asking your child to describe her feelings will affirm her as a person and tell her that you care about her. Always teach your child that her feelings matter, instead of immediately assuming that her fears are "strange" or "wrong." You may not like the fact that she's afraid, or you may want to dismiss her feelings because they're blocking your agenda, but empathizing with her will mean she'll rebel less.

Don't shame. Don't say,

> *"You embarrass me when you make a fuss at the stylist's."*

Never tell your child that she embarrasses you. Doing so will only increase her fears, and it may become a self-fulfilling prophecy.

Instead, be positive. Say,

> *"I'm sorry you don't like getting a haircut.*
> *Let's think of ways you can have fun while your hair is getting cut."*

Teach your child to develop the attitude that every challenge is an opportunity to find solutions. Encourage her to play a game with you while she's getting her hair cut ("I Spy," for example).

Don't name-call. Don't say,

> *"What do you mean you're afraid? Why are you such a wimp?"*

How would you like it if someone said this to you? Humiliating your child will only increase her fears and will teach her to make fun of others when they're afraid. You want to avoid these outcomes at all costs.

Instead, affirm your child's feelings. Say,

> *"I understand that you're feeling afraid when you're getting your*
> *hair cut, but I know you're brave and strong and can handle it."*

Affirming your child's bravery will help her become more confident and resilient.

Chapter Thirty-six

"Let's Change Your Diaper."
"No! I Don't Wanna Get My Diaper Changed!"

What two-year-old wants to stop playing just to get his diaper changed? Since this hassle probably doesn't seem necessary to your child, it's your job to sell the experience as an exercise in cooperation. Some activities are wants; this one's a need. Teaching your child the difference is a must-do part of being a caring parent.

Helpful Hints

✋ Monitor diaper rash and other physical problems that might make diaper changing painful for your child. Treat the problem immediately or consult your physician.

✋ Entertain your child with songs and nursery rhymes during changing, or give him a special toy to play with.

Self-Talk

Don't tell yourself,
"I don't want to do this, either. Why is he making it so hard?"
This negative attitude spells trouble. Seeing yourself as a victim will communicate to your child that *he's* to blame for making your life miserable. When he senses your resentment, he'll be less likely to comply with your wishes because he'll want to avoid you at all costs.

Instead, tell yourself,
"I can handle a few more months of diaper changing even if it's a struggle sometimes."
This affirmation will help you manage your child's resistance with less stress. When you're calm and patient, you're able to take a "no big deal" attitude toward your child's wriggling during changes.

Don't tell yourself,

> *"I'll just let him wear his wet diaper until*
> *his bottom is so sore he'll want it changed."*

This kind of thinking is hazardous to your child's health. Never let yourself think that it's okay for your child to suffer physical harm as a consequence of his resistance.

Instead, tell yourself,

> *"I understand why my child doesn't want me to change his diaper.*
> *I don't need to get upset over this."*

When your child doesn't want to cooperate, interpreting his behavior as *his* problem, not yours, helps you focus on his feelings instead of yours. It's easier to teach him to cooperate when anger isn't shutting down your ability to problem solve.

Don't tell yourself,

> *"I've got to get him changed before my mother-in-law gets here,*
> *or she'll think I'm a bad parent."*

Change your child's diaper when he needs it, not because someone else will judge you if you don't. Your focus should be on your child's needs, not on someone else's opinion of you.

Instead, tell yourself,

> *"I don't care what my mother-in-law thinks about my parenting decisions."*

Don't think about the outside pressures to care for your child a certain way. Doing so lets you follow your child's needs, not someone else's.

Talking to Your Child

Don't threaten. Don't say,

> *"Stop wiggling and yelling or I'll smack your bare bottom!"*

When you're frustrated and angry, these kinds of threats may seem like good ways to gain your child's cooperation. However, they simply increase your child's fears, making him scream more or freeze up to avoid making you mad. Neither teaches him to do what you ask.

Instead, empathize. Say,

> *"I know you don't want to get changed now, but we have to.*
> *Let's do it quickly so you can get back to your toys."*

Gently helping your child focus on the fun that's coming can encourage him to cooperate. In addition, making diaper changing a fun experience will help reduce his resistance. Frame the situation as an opportunity to cuddle, tickle, and love your child—not hurt him.

Don't get angry. Don't say,

"You're making me mad. Now hold still so I can change you!"

Your child isn't responsible for your anger. You are! Getting mad won't teach him to cooperate; it will only increase his resistance.

Instead, empathize. Say,

"I'm sorry you don't want to get your diaper changed, but we have to do it because it's important to keep your bottom clean."

Stick to your agenda while empathizing with your child's feelings. Doing so models compassion and responsibility. Your child will trust you when you tell him how good it feels to be clean and dry, and he'll believe you when your explanation proves true.

Don't bribe. Don't say,

"I'll give you a cookie if you let me change you."

Bribing your child will teach him that he should get a reward for cooperating.

Instead, make a deal. Say,

"When we're finished changing your diaper, then we can go to the park."

Both of you can meet your agendas when you follow Grandma's Rule, which teaches your child to meet his obligations before doing fun activities. Making a deal with your child is your ticket to a win-win relationship.

Don't give up. Don't say,

"Fine. I'm not going to fight with you. I won't change you until your bottom is sore. Then you'll be sorry."

Never threaten dire consequences to motivate your toddler to cooperate. Giving up not only teaches him to fold in the face of resistance, it tells him you don't care enough about him to help him avoid the pain of diaper rash.

Instead, teach the lesson. Say,

"Letting me change you now will keep your bottom from getting sore."

Help your child understand the consequences of diaper changing. Explain the benefits of being clean and dry so he knows you have his best interests in mind and that you're not arbitrarily taking him away from his play. Treat him as you would want to be treated.

Chapter Thirty-seven

"Please Wash Your Hands."
"No! I Don't Wanna Wash My Hands!"

For toddlers and preschoolers in particular, hand washing can be a difficult task. The water comes on too fast, they can't reach the faucet, the soap won't stay in their hands, they can't get the soap dispenser to work, and so on. No wonder young children resist hand washing. Although your sink may not be designed with your preschooler in mind, she still needs to learn the skill. Make sure she develops this important habit by making it a nonnegotiable part of her cleanup routine.

Helpful Hints

🖐 Make rules about when and how often your child must wash her hands.

🖐 Put a step stool in every bathroom in your home so your child can reach the sink safely without your help.

🖐 Make sure your water heater is set no higher than 120°F to prevent the water from scalding your child's hands.

🖐 Model good hand-washing habits and comment on the importance of staying clean and healthy.

🖐 Supervise your child's hand washing to ensure she's using the soap and water properly. Don't forget to praise her for a job well done.

🖐 Avoid frightening your child with tales of dangerous bugs or germs living on her skin.

Self-Talk

Don't tell yourself,

"When is my child going to learn to wash her hands without my having to remind her?"

Even though the need for repeated reminders may frustrate you, stay positive. It takes lots of practice to perfect the fine art of hand washing.

Instead, tell yourself,

> *"I can handle reminding my child to wash her hands."*

Providing gentle reminders doesn't have to be a negative experience; you can do it pleasantly and empathetically. Affirming your ability to cope with your child's refusals gives you the strength to remain calm in the face of adversity.

Don't tell yourself,

> *"I'm sick and tired of trying to get her to wash her hands before dinner. I'll just wash them when I give her a bath."*

Don't throw in the towel! Giving up on teaching hand washing can be a health hazard and won't teach your child a valuable hygiene habit.

Instead, tell yourself,

> *"I understand my child's reluctance to wash her hands. It's hard for her to turn on the faucet and get the soap off her hands."*

Empathizing with your child's difficulties will encourage her cooperation. Let her know that you sometimes have trouble getting the soap off, too, but you persevere until it's done.

Don't tell yourself,

> *"If I don't make her wash her hands, she'll be sick all the time."*

Don't exaggerate the possible consequences. Fearing the worst will increase your anxiety and make you exert undue pressure to get your child to wash her hands. Teaching through fear is a negative way to accomplish what can be done positively.

Instead, tell yourself,

> *"I need to keep the hygiene goal in mind even when she balks at washing her hands."*

Staying focused on your long-term goal can help you cope with short-term resistance. Keep the goal in mind while teaching—not dictating—good hygiene habits.

Talking to Your Child

Don't whine. Don't say,

> *"I asked you nicely six times. Now get in there and do it!"*

Remember that your child may need a few reminders before she gets the job done. Complaining about that fact will only encourage her to tune you out completely.

Instead, remind her about the rule. Say,

"What's the rule about washing hands when you go to the bathroom?"

Asking your child to tell you the rule reminds her of what to do and reinforces the habit. Eventually your reminders will disappear as the behavior becomes automatic.

Don't threaten. Don't say,

"If you can't cooperate and wash your hands, you'll have to sit in time-out."

Putting your child in time-out for refusing to wash her hands will make hand washing even less appealing and won't teach her to enjoy this important habit. In addition, she won't learn to wash her hands while sitting in time-out.

Instead, praise cooperative behavior. Say,

"Thank you for going in the bathroom to wash your hands. I'll help you turn on the faucet if you want."

Praising your child's progress will remind her of the goal and will encourage her to see it through to completion.

Don't give up. Don't say,

"I don't care if you don't wash your hands, but you'll be sorry when you get sick."

Your lack of caring sends your child a hurtful message and doesn't help her understand the connection between hand washing and illness. Withholding your love may motivate her to comply in the short term, but it won't teach her the long-term value of cooperation. Your child needs to know that your love is unconditional.

Instead, remind her about the rule. Say,

"I understand that it may be frustrating to wash hands when you're really hungry, but the rule says we need to do that before eating."

Stick to the rule while modeling empathy and persistence. Your child will pick up on the lessons from this teachable moment.

Chapter Thirty-eight

"It's Time to Cut Your Nails."
"No! I Don't Want You to Cut My Nails!"

Nail-trimming fears often begin during the early years when one close call is enough to convince your child that it's not a pleasant experience. To counteract your child's resistance, let him watch you trim your nails so he can see that the procedure is safe. You can also play manicuring games to lower his anxiety about nail trimming. Make nail trimming a part of his cleanup routine, so he knows that it's another nonnegotiable task he needs to complete.

Helpful Hints

✋ Choose a time for nail trimming that doesn't interrupt your child's favorite activity, such as after a bath or before bed.

✋ Avoid trying to trim your child's nails when he's tired or hungry. It'll be harder for him to sit still then, which will increase the chances of an accidental "owie."

Self-Talk

Don't tell yourself,
"He has to do what I tell him to do...right now!"
Demanding immediate compliance from your child will lead to war. Reframe the situation as something you'd *like* him to do, which allows you to take a softer, more empathetic approach to gaining his cooperation.

Instead, tell yourself,
"Demanding that my child cooperate won't make the situation any easier."
Understand that attempting to exert authoritarian control over your child will backfire. Instead, figure out ways to let him actively participate in the process. For example, ask him to hold the clippers while you're preparing to clip his nails.

Don't tell yourself,

"My child is so stubborn that it's hard to like him at times."

It's important to separate your child from his behavior. You may not like his refusal to cooperate, but you love him unconditionally. Make sure he knows that.

Instead, tell yourself,

"I may not like his resistance when I try to trim his nails, but I'll always adore my child."

Say these words over and over whenever you find yourself getting upset about your child's defiance. It'll help you remember what's most important.

Don't tell yourself,

"I don't care if his nails don't get trimmed. He can just chew them off for all I care."

Giving up will show your child how to shirk his responsibilities when faced with adversity. It will also encourage him to develop the bad habit of chewing his nails.

Instead, tell yourself,

"It's important to use empathy and patience when helping my child learn to take care of himself."

Although your child's agenda may not match yours, stay your course. It's your job to be empathetic and patient.

Don't tell yourself,

"What if my mother sees my child's long nails? She'll think I'm neglecting him."

Try to remember that you base your decisions about your child on what you believe is right for him. Repeat this fact to yourself often (and to anyone else, if necessary) to bolster your confidence.

Instead, tell yourself,

"It's no big deal if my mother thinks my child's nails are too long."

Yielding to social pressure may make you demand your child's compliance instead of adopting positive strategies to gain his cooperation. In your role as parent, you must learn to rely on your instincts and experience when dealing with your child.

Talking to Your Child

Don't be aggressive. Don't say,
"I'm going to cut your nails whether you like it or not. Now hold still."
This kind of dictatorial parenting hurts everyone involved. Chances are your child will resist even more if you try to hold him down.

Instead, invite feedback. Say,
"Help me understand why you don't want to have your nails trimmed."
Asking your child why he's resisting will not only help you understand his thinking, it will validate him as a person. Both consequences will encourage his cooperation. When you find out what's bothering him, you'll have a better chance of fixing the problem and getting the job done.

Don't threaten. Don't say,
"If you don't let me cut your nails,
you'll have to spend the rest of the day in your room."
Threatening to isolate your child won't teach him how to do what he needs to do. It will only hurt your relationship and teach him that he'll be punished for not doing what you ask. When he doesn't cooperate, he needs you to teach him how to complete the task and motivate him to follow your direction.

Instead, play a game. Say,
"Let's play the manicure game.
I'll get the table ready so we can trim your nails."
Making a game out of cutting your child's nails will make the task fun. You can accomplish anything with your child when you love and laugh together through the experience.

Don't use fear. Don't say,
"If you don't let me cut your nails, they'll get long and
scratch somebody, and then you'll be in big trouble."
Threatening your child with adverse social consequences may frighten him into doing what you ask, but it won't teach him the proper reason for cooperating.

Instead, empathize. Say,
"It's important to keep our nails trimmed so we don't
accidentally scratch someone. We don't want that to happen."
Appeal to your child's innate empathy to help him understand the importance of keeping his nails trimmed for his own safety as well as the safety of others.

Chapter Thirty-nine

"Let's Wash Your Hair."
"No! I Don't Wanna Get My Hair Washed!"

Soap in the eyes. Soap in the ears. Soap in the mouth. What good is all this hair washing anyway? To your three-year-old, the thought of clean hair does little to help her endure the muss and fuss of shampooing. When you hear a plaintive cry such as, "Don't sham my poo!" find out what part of the process upsets her. Then try to solve the problem without compromising the goal.

Helpful Hints

❧ Wash your child's hair before she hits the "too tired" mark, and do it first thing when she gets in the tub so you can get it out of the way.

❧ Let your child pick out her shampoo (within limits) so she can have some control over the situation.

❧ Encourage her to hold a towel or washcloth over her eyes and ears to prevent water and soap from getting in.

❧ Allow her to rinse her hair with the shower wand or rinsing bucket so she can take an active role in the process.

Self-Talk

Don't tell yourself,
"My child drives me crazy with her constant fussing about shampooing."
Making your child responsible for your mood prevents you from taking control of your feelings.

Instead, tell yourself,
"Getting upset won't help either of us."
Keeping yourself calm helps both of you learn about self-control. Think of hair washing as an opportunity to make bubbles and crazy hairdos instead of tears.

Don't tell yourself,
"I'm tired of the battles. I don't care if she ever gets her hair washed."
Don't avoid the task just because your child is resisting it. Giving up is not only bad for her health, it shows her how to quit when faced with adversity.

Instead, tell yourself,
"My goal is to help my child learn to cope with things she doesn't like."
Keeping your long-term goal in mind will help you manage your child's resistance and find ways of eliciting her cooperation. This is not just about shampooing; it's about you and your child finding ways to work as a team.

_____

Don't tell yourself,
"I've got to shampoo my child's hair before my mother sees it. She always criticizes me if it's dirty."
Doing something to please someone else puts you under considerable pressure to perform. It doesn't help you do what's best for your child. Keep your mother out of your hair (and your child's, too).

Instead, tell yourself,
"I'm growing as a parent when I help my child learn to cope with shampooing."
Helping your child learn to cooperate is a good way to learn new ways to cope yourself. One of the gifts of parenthood is that our children teach us ways to handle life's challenges, as we help them do the same.

_____

Don't tell yourself,
"Why can't she just cooperate? I'm too stressed-out to put up with this nonsense."
Demanding cooperation from your preschooler is bound to fail. She's designed to meet her own needs and not worry about yours. Understanding that her behavior is developmentally appropriate will go far to reduce your stress.

Instead, tell yourself,
"I know it can be scary for her to have water and shampoo running down her face."
Your empathy will help you communicate with patience and love, two qualities that will help your child endure this chore.

Talking to Your Child

Don't be disrespectful. Don't say,

"I don't care if you're afraid of the soap and water. That's just too bad."

Even though you may be determined to wash your child's hair even if she protests, don't use this type of language. Your lack of empathy tells her that you won't support her when she's upset or afraid.

Instead, be helpful. Say,

"I understand that you don't like shampooing, but we have to get your hair clean. I'll be gentle and try to keep it from getting in your eyes."

Teach your child that you're on her side. Anything's possible when she has your support.

Don't discount her feelings. Don't say,

"What are you crying about? Don't be so silly.
I'm just going to shampoo your hair."

Your child may believe she's about to be hurt, so telling her that she's being silly discounts her feelings and increases her resistance. It also tells her that your love depends on her doing what you want her to do, another hurtful message that will damage your relationship and her motivation to cooperate.

Instead, offer solutions. Say,

"I understand that you're afraid of getting soap in your eyes.
Hold this washcloth over your eyes so the shampoo won't get in."

Tell your child that you understand her fears and that you'll protect her from harm—then make sure to follow through.

Don't bribe. Don't say,

"If you let me shampoo your hair, I'll give you a sucker."

Bribing your child teaches her to expect a reward for cooperating, rather than teaching her the value of cooperation. Bribing may produce short-term results, but it doesn't build long-term habits or help your child develop cooperative behaviors.

Instead, use Grandma's Rule. Say,

"When I've finished shampooing your hair,
then you may play with your tub toys for a while."

Grandma's Rule teaches your child that work comes before play, and that accepting responsibilities makes everyone happy.

Chapter Forty

"You Need to Wipe Your Nose."
"No! I Don't Wanna Wipe My Nose!"

You can't believe your ears. Of all the things your three-year-old doesn't want to do, why is wiping his nose one of them? Your child might tell you that it's scary ("My nose might come off!"), disgusting ("It's so gross!"), or uncomfortable ("Ouch! It hurts!"). Whatever his reaction, your job is to gently encourage him to learn another important skill. Eventually, his fear will go away, just like his runny nose.

Helpful Hints

🖐 Make sure you have the softest tissues available.

🖐 Keep tissues in handy locations so your child can learn to help himself when he needs one.

🖐 Model how to blow your nose properly so he can learn how to do it.

Self-Talk

Don't tell yourself,
"What's so hard about wiping your nose?"
Being unable or unwilling to see the world from your child's point of view will prevent you from helping him learn to cooperate.

Instead, tell yourself,
"I understand his reluctance to wipe his nose when it's so red and sore."
Appreciate where your child is coming from. When he knows you're on his side, he'll be more inclined to follow your directions.

Don't tell yourself,
"I don't care if he's got snot running down his face.
I'm tired of fighting with him about wiping his nose."
You can view parenting as a relentless cycle of annoyances and aggravations, or you can see it as a series of interesting lessons about human behavior. Choosing the latter perspective will be more helpful in teaching your child to cooperate.

Instead, tell yourself,

> *"I need to stay focused on the long-term goal of*
> *helping my child develop good hygiene habits."*

Reminding yourself of the goal can prevent you from getting upset about minor skirmishes. Your agenda is to help your child learn the fine art of nose wiping. His agenda is to avoid any pain or discomfort. Working together will help you meet both agendas.

Don't tell yourself,

> *"What will people think of me when they*
> *see my child with snot all over his face?"*

Stay focused on what's most important for your child, not on what other people think. If his nose is running faster than he can wipe it, so be it. Avoid being paranoid about how others judge your family.

Instead, tell yourself,

> *"I can't be concerned about what others think."*

Keeping the imagined thoughts of others out of your mind will keep your stress level down. If you stay calm and relaxed, your child will likely do the same. You'll be a more effective teacher, and he'll be in a better frame of mind to learn.

Talking to Your Child

Don't shame. Don't say,

> *"Your nose is disgusting. Now get a tissue and wipe it!"*

Don't tell your child that his nose disgusts you, even if it does. It's important to keep negative opinions to yourself to avoid hurting his feelings. Using putdowns only models bad behavior and doesn't accomplish the goal.

Instead, empathize. Say,

> *"I understand that you don't want to wipe your nose.*
> *But when it runs, you can spread germs and make your lip sore."*

There's no reason to have a power struggle. Just keep a box of tissues handy, continue to help your child wipe or blow his nose, and pour on the TLC. Everyone will feel better.

Don't nag. Don't say,

> *"How many times do I have to tell you to wipe your nose?*
> *Now get in there and do it!"*

Although frustration may tempt you to ask your child this unanswerable question, don't do it. It will only send him the unkind message that he's a burden to you; it won't teach him to cooperate.

Instead, teach the skill. Say,

> *"Let me show you how to blow your nose gently*
> *so it doesn't get redder and more irritated."*

Focus on the solution, not the problem. Your offer to be careful and your awareness of your child's sore nose let him know that you care about his feelings.

Don't threaten. Don't say,

> *"If I have to come over there and wipe your nose, you'll be sorry."*

Don't threaten your child to get him to take care of himself. You'll only tempt him to call your bluff, which will force you to follow through with a negative consequence. Getting your attention—positive or negative—is the prize he covets most, so don't tempt him to avoid cooperating just to get your attention.

Instead, make a deal. Say,

> *"When you wipe your nose, then you can go back to playing."*

Children don't want to be interrupted when they're playing, so promise your child that he can meet his agenda after he's met yours.

Don't use fear. Don't say,

> *"Nobody will like you if you have a runny nose."*

Don't tell your child lies to shock him into cooperating. Doing so teaches him to exaggerate to get someone's attention. Threatening him with social isolation won't motivate him to practice good hygiene.

Instead, praise cooperative behavior. Say,

> *"Thank you for getting a tissue.*
> *Your nose will feel much better when it's wiped."*

Praising your child for *any* cooperation encourages him to continue the behavior. Positive attention will make him feel proud of his accomplishment.

Chapter Forty-one

"Let's Fix Your Hair."
"No! I Don't Want You to Fix My Hair!"

The day starts in perfect harmony until you mention that your three-year-old's hair needs to be fixed. She screams! She runs away from you! The battle begins! Avoid this power struggle by teaching her how to adopt a new attitude toward grooming. You can relate to the fact that she doesn't want to sit still or endure the pain of a scratchy barrette, so find ways for her to help decide which barrette to use, where it should go, whether to use a comb or a brush, and so on. Be her ally, not her enemy, as you teach her good grooming habits.

Helpful Hints

ψ Make a rule that your child's hair needs to be brushed or combed every day.

ψ Allow ample time to fix your child's hair so you can avoid hurrying.

ψ Select combs and brushes that are easy to use.

ψ Let your child participate in decisions about her hairstyle.

Self-Talk

Don't tell yourself,
"I don't want my child to be mad at me, so I'll never fix her hair again."
Empathizing with your child is good, but don't let it interfere with what's best for her. Avoid the "all or nothing" approach when your child protests your efforts. Her resistance is not about you; it's about not having enough control (or about the brush hurting her scalp).

Instead, tell yourself,
"I will not rate myself as a parent by how mad or glad my child is about the rules I set for her."
Keep your parenting self-esteem separate from your child's behavior. Doing so will prevent unneeded anxiety and will help you maintain a

relaxed approach to managing your child's protests. She may not always love the rules, but she loves you.

Don't tell yourself,

> *"My child would look so cute if she'd let me
> do her hair like my mother did mine."*

It's fine to encourage a cute hairstyle, but avoid comparing yourself to your child. What worked for you may not please her.

Instead, tell yourself,

> *"Just because I loved having a ponytail doesn't mean my child has to."*

Your child is not you, so her likes and dislikes won't be the same as yours. Make suggestions, but let her decide what works best for her.

Don't tell yourself,

> *"I can't let her go to preschool with her hair looking like that."*

Worrying about what your child's teacher thinks is a waste of time. What matters most is what your child thinks about her hair.

Instead, tell yourself,

> *"My child needs to learn how to make decisions about her hair."*

Understanding your child's need to make her own decisions can help you prepare her to make smart decisions for the rest of her life. Listen to her opinions and validate them whenever possible. It's *her* hair, not yours. Help her celebrate that fact.

Talking to Your Child

Don't use guilt. Don't say,

> *"I can't wait for you to have a daughter who
> makes a fuss about her hair like you do."*

Dire predictions won't teach your child to cooperate; rather, they'll send her the unhealthy message that her actions must always please you.

Instead, remind her about the rule. Say,

> *"The rule says that your hair needs
> to be fixed before you go to your dad's."*

Using the rule as the enforcer lets your child focus on the rule, not you.

Don't make it personal. Don't say,
> *"I guess I can't do anything right."*

Your child's refusal to cooperate isn't a statement about your parenting or hairstyling skills. It simply means that she wants some say in how her hair is done.

Instead, make it a game. Say,
> *"Let's play beauty shop. You fix my hair, and I'll fix yours."*

Making hair grooming a fun game will reduce conflict and let your child actively participate in both the decision making and hairstyling.

Don't belittle. Don't say,
> *"Fine! Wear that stupid barrette. I don't care if you look silly."*

Don't give up on trying to help your child improve her grooming habits. Giving up tells her that it's okay to quit when things don't go your way.

Instead, praise cooperative behavior. Say,
> *"Thanks for sitting so still while I fix your hair."*

Praising your child's compliance encourages her to cooperate more in the future. Nothing motivates your child more than your approval and support.

Don't use anger. Don't say,
> *"Stop yelling! You're really making me mad!"*

Telling your child that her resistance is responsible for your anger diminishes her ability to empathize with others. She won't understand your position because she'll naturally try to defend herself by blaming you for hurting her in the first place. Remember, *you* control whether or not you get angry.

Instead, make a deal. Say,
> *"When we've finished brushing your hair,*
> *then you may play with your toys."*

This use of Grandma's Rule teaches your child that she must do what's necessary before she gets to do what she wants. It also teaches her that cooperation is a win-win proposition. You both feel good when your agendas are met, a lesson she'll find useful throughout her life.

SECTION VII
EDUCATION

The greatest discovery of my generation
is that human beings can alter their lives
by altering their attitudes.

—*William James*

Chapter Forty-two

"It's Time to Go to Preschool."
"No! I Don't Wanna Go to Preschool!"

Your child's preschool boycott can take various forms: wanting to stay in bed, complaining about stomachaches, whining about teachers and classmates who are "mean" or who "don't like him," and so on. Listen to his complaints carefully and talk to his teacher to find out if there's a problem. When he knows you'll support him, he'll feel comfortable asking for help. And if he knows you'll take his concerns seriously, he'll be more inclined to cooperate.

Helpful Hints

🖐 Before enrolling your child in a preschool, take him for a visit to ensure a good fit. Interview the director and teachers, discuss the educational philosophy, and observe a class.

🖐 Let your child spend some time away from you, even for short periods, so he'll get used to not being with you all the time.

🖐 Stay in close contact with your child's teachers so you can deal with minor problems before they become serious.

🖐 Talk about *getting* to go to preschool, rather than *having* to go.

🖐 Make rules so your child understands which days he goes to school and which days he stays home.

Self-Talk

Don't tell yourself,
"What's the matter with him? He makes a fuss about everything."
Exaggerating the problem only makes you feel overwhelmed and helpless.

Instead, tell yourself,

> **"I understand his desire to stay home.**
> **I'd rather stay home, too, sometimes."**

Your child is more likely to cooperate with someone who understands his feelings.

Don't tell yourself,

> **"He makes me feel guilty when I have to work**
> **and he has to go to preschool."**

Feeling guilty because you work won't help you or your child cope with separation. Guilt comes from thinking you've done something wrong. Instead, remind yourself that working and sending your child to preschool are in your family's best interests. In addition, avoid blaming your child for feelings *you* create.

Instead, tell yourself,

> **"Even though I miss him when he's in preschool,**
> **I'm happy that we're able to send him."**

When you tell yourself that you're grateful for your child's opportunity, you send the same message to your child. Your enthusiasm will be contagious.

Don't tell yourself,

> **"What will his teachers think if I don't make him go to school?"**

Worrying starts with a "what if" question that leads to endless speculation about what might happen in situations beyond your control.

Instead, tell yourself,

> **"My goal is to help my child love learning."**

The teachers share your desire to promote your child's educational and social development, so engage them as allies. Keeping your long-term goals in mind can help you overcome your child's resistance.

Don't tell yourself,

> **"I can't stand hearing him cry, so I'll just let him stay home."**

Giving in will teach your child that making a fuss will get him what he wants.

Instead, tell yourself,

> **"My child's resistance to preschool doesn't mean he doesn't love learning."**

Keep the problem in perspective. Adjusting to preschool is a big challenge for most kids.

Talking to Your Child

Don't shame. Don't say,

> *"What do you mean you don't want to go to preschool?*
> *I paid good money so you could go!"*

Shaming your child into compliance by reminding him of your sacrifice won't resolve what's bothering him. Instead, it will create resentment toward you.

Instead, invite feedback. Say,

> *"Help me understand why you don't want to go to preschool."*

Asking your child to explain his fears not only tells him you care about him, it helps you identify the problem and solve it.

Don't demand. Don't say,

> *"You're going to preschool whether you like it or not.*
> *Now get yourself ready."*

Demanding that your child comply is bound to fail because it assumes you can control his behavior. You can't. Your refusal to empathize tells him you don't care about his feelings.

Instead, shift the focus. Say,

> *"Think about all the fun you'll have at preschool.*
> *You'll miss that if you don't go."*

Helping your child focus on the future fun will make the immediate problem seem less significant. Shifting his focus will help him see the situation in a new light.

Don't give in. Don't say,

> *"Okay, stay home. I don't care if you ever go to school."*

Telling your child that you don't care about him or his education will teach him not to care and to give up when faced with adversity. You may think that giving in will help him be happy, but what he really needs is to resolve his fears about going to school.

Instead, be positive. Say,

"We're all going to our jobs today. I'm going to mine and you're going to yours at preschool. We'll see each other after work."

Putting a positive spin on your time apart can help you both cope with separation more easily. Your child will pick up on your empathy and team approach, which will help him understand that you have something in common—the important responsibility of doing your jobs.

Don't bribe. Don't say,

"If you go to preschool today, I'll get you a new toy to play with when you get home."

Bribing your child tells him that he should expect a material reward for doing what you ask. The reward of fun with friends and a caring teacher should be all the motivation he needs.

Instead, make a deal. Say,

"I know you want to play with puzzles this morning. When you go to preschool, then you can ask your teacher if you can play with puzzles."

Use Grandma's Rule to motivate your child and remind him that when he does what he has to do, then he gets to do what he wants to do (within limits, of course).

Don't threaten. Don't say,

"If you don't go to preschool, you'll grow up to be stupid."

This hurtful prediction will actually increase your child's anxiety about going to school.

Instead, remind him about the rule. Say,

"I understand that you don't want to go to preschool, but the rule says that you go on Monday, Wednesday, and Friday. Today is Wednesday, so let's get ready."

By lovingly invoking the rule, you're telling your child that you care about him even when the rule tells him to do something he doesn't like.

Chapter Forty-three

"You're Going to a New Preschool."
"No! I Don't Wanna Go to a New Preschool!"

Your child may not protest so directly, but you may notice other signs that she doesn't like the idea of going to a new preschool: She may not want to talk about it, she may have a tantrum on her way to school, she may act aggressively toward other children, or she may tell you her tummy hurts when you bring up the subject. All of these signs are clues that she needs to practice adjusting to change.

Helpful Hints

✋ Emphasize the positive aspects of the new school, such as a larger playground, more kids her age, closer to home, and so on.

✋ Before changing schools, visit the new school with your child to show her the environment and to warn her that a change is imminent.

Self-Talk

Don't tell yourself,
"My child is so shy, she'll never be able to cope with change."
Your child is learning to adapt to new situations; labeling her as shy may discourage you from helping her make a necessary change.

Instead, tell yourself,
"I know this is tough for my child,
but I'm sure she can manage the change."
Empathizing with your child's fears and affirming her ability to work through them keeps your mind open to ways of helping her cope.

Don't tell yourself,
"I can't cope with any more stress. Having to move is hard enough."
Telling yourself that you can't cope shuts down your ability to solve problems creatively. Negative messages aren't healthy for you or your child.

Instead, tell yourself,

"As I help her cope with change, I'm learning new ways of coping myself."
Sometimes teaching your child helps you learn things about yourself.
View the challenge as an opportunity for both of you to grow.

Don't tell yourself,

"I'll be so embarrassed if she has a meltdown in front of her new teacher."
Don't let your child's meltdown embarrass you. Doing so says that
you're responsible for her emotions and that you care more about
how you appear to others than how she feels.

Instead, tell yourself,

"Although I feel guilty about having to change schools,
I know it's best for her right now."
Acknowledging your feelings of guilt and telling yourself that your
decisions are in your child's best interests will help you cope.

Don't tell yourself,

"My child's refusal to go to a new school is a disaster!"
Exaggerating the problem can make it seem unfixable. Remember,
all events are neutral; how you think about them makes them
positive or negative.

Instead, tell yourself,

"My goal is to help her learn to cope with change."
Keeping this larger goal in mind will make changing schools an
opportunity to teach her to be flexible.

Talking to Your Child

Don't use guilt. Don't say,

"You know we can't afford to send you to your old school,
so you have to go to this one."
Avoid telling your child that her needs are too expensive. Doing so makes
her responsible for a situation that's beyond her control. In addition,
your lack of empathy tells her that you don't care about her feelings.

Instead, praise cooperative behavior. Say,

"I know it's hard to make a change,
but you're brave and strong and I know you can do it."
Affirming your child's bravery can help her gain the strength she needs
to cope with change. Your words can create a self-fulfilling prophecy.

Don't bribe. Don't say,

> *"If you'll go to your new school without complaining,*
> *I'll buy you a new bike."*

Bribing your child teaches her that she can get a reward for doing something she doesn't want to do.

Instead, make a deal. Say,

> *"After you go to school, then we can have a friend over to play."*

Grandma's Rule helps your child focus on the positive consequence of following your directions, and teaches her to take care of her responsibilities before following her agenda.

Don't blame. Don't say,

> *"I don't care what you want. Your dad isn't paying*
> *enough child support for you to stay in your old preschool."*

Don't dismiss your child's feelings and blame your ex for having to change preschools. Doing so will teach your child that her feelings don't matter. It will also test her loyalty to each parent and increase the tension between you and your ex.

Instead, be proactive. Say,

> *"I know you don't want to go to a new school, but this one is*
> *closer to my job and I can have lunch with you once in a while."*

Helping your child focus on the benefits of changing schools will teach her to tolerate frustration and be flexible.

Don't label. Don't say,

> *"I know you're shy and have trouble making friends,*
> *but you still have to go to the new school."*

Telling your child she's shy makes her problem permanent. Her behavior doesn't define her; it can always change.

Instead, be supportive. Say,

> *"We're going to visit your new school today.*
> *I think you'll really like it and make friends there."*

Provide emotional support for your child and affirm her ability to make friends while she investigates a new school. Your positive attitude will help her accept that change is a normal part of life.

Chapter Forty-four

"Please Listen to Your Teacher."
"No! I Don't Wanna Listen to My Teacher!"

When you get a report that your three-year-old isn't listening or following directions at school, the teacher's observations may reveal important information about the fit between your child and his teacher. Is your child frequently inattentive, oppositional, and bored? Is he angry about having to go to school? Are issues from his home life, such as adapting to a new sibling, affecting his behavior at school? Work closely with the teacher to understand how your child learns best and to send your child consistent messages to motivate cooperative behavior.

Helpful Hints

🖐 Stress to your child the importance of showing respect to teachers and others.

🖐 Tell your child how much you appreciated your teachers when you were in school.

🖐 Treat your child with the respect you expect him to show his teachers.

🖐 Model empathy, kindness, caring, and courtesy.

Self-Talk

Don't tell yourself,
"I'm so embarrassed when my child's teacher tells me he's not listening to her."
Feeling embarrassed suggests that you're responsible for your child's behavior. You're responsible for *teaching* him; he's responsible for doing what you've taught.

Instead, tell yourself,
"I know his teacher understands that my child's listening problem isn't my fault."
Your child's teacher understands that occasionally uncooperative behavior is developmentally appropriate for preschoolers.

Don't tell yourself,

> *"I get so disgusted with him when he doesn't listen to his teacher."*

Your disgust tells your child that you're having problems separating him from his behavior. He needs to know that your love is unconditional—that you love him even when you don't like his behavior.

Instead, tell yourself,

> *"I don't like that my child isn't listening or following directions in school, but we can solve the problem."*

Telling yourself you don't like something helps you express your emotions, then lets you get on with the task of solving the problem.

Don't tell yourself,

> *"Why can't my child just listen and follow directions?"*

Every parent would love to have a polite, obedient child. But normal, healthy children often don't want to do something, even though they can.

Instead, tell yourself,

> *"My goal is to help my child learn to follow the rules and do his best."*

Keeping your long-term goal in mind helps you focus on helping your child succeed.

Don't tell yourself,

> *"If he can't learn to sit down and shut up at school, he'll never learn anything."*

Don't make dire predictions about your child's ability to learn. Doing so creates needless stress and prevents you from finding ways to help him learn.

Instead, tell yourself,

> *"Learning is a process, and I need to be patient with my child."*

Think about the situation as a teachable moment, and remember that learning to learn takes time and perseverance.

Talking to Your Child

Don't threaten. Don't say,

> *"Every time your teacher tells me you aren't listening or following directions, you're going to get a spanking!"*

Threatening to hurt your child will make him fear you and his teachers. It won't help him learn to cooperate.

Instead, invite feedback. Say,

"Tell me about listening and following directions in school.
I want to know what makes it so hard to do."

Ask your child to tell you about his views on certain tasks, but avoid the confrontational *why*. His response will give you insight into his behavior and will help you find ways to solve the problem.

Don't label. Don't say,

"What's the matter with you? I thought you were smart enough to listen!"

Don't tell your child that something is wrong with him because he doesn't choose to listen or follow directions in school. Doing so won't help him learn how to do those tasks and will encourage him to feel bad about himself.

Instead, offer support. Say,

"It's important to listen to your teacher.
Let's talk about ways you can do that."

Letting your child help solve the problem validates him and makes him part of the solution. It also focuses attention on the goal, not on his unwillingness to cooperate.

Don't shame. Don't say,

"I'm so ashamed of you. I've told you time and
again to listen to your teacher, but you just don't get it."

Trying to motivate your child by shaming him tells him that your love is conditional. If he learns to do tasks only to avoid shame, fear and anxiety will motivate him, which can cause depression and lack of confidence.

Instead, reinforce teamwork. Say,

"I'm going to meet with your teacher today so we can
find ways to help you listen and follow directions in school."

Working with your child's teacher will help you discover whether your child can't hear, is bored, or fears failure. When you find the underlying problem, you can take steps to help your child. Telling him that you want to be on his team sends him the message that you care about him.

Chapter Forty-five

"Today You'll Be in the Little Kids' Room." "No! I Don't Wanna Be in the Little Kids' Room!"

One day your four-year-old is behaving like a senior account manager, getting along well with the his underlings; the next day she wants nothing to do with her junior associates, including being in the same room with them. Don't let her fickleness drive you to distraction. Simply tell her about the rules governing room assignments, so she'll know that she was placed in the room that's best for her.

Helpful Hints

✋ Enlist your child's preschool teacher in helping her adjust to her room assignment.

✋ Make sure her activities are stimulating and appropriate for her ability.

Self-Talk

Don't tell yourself,

"I'll talk to the people in charge and get my child moved to another room."

Although you may be tempted to rescue your child from her "suffering," fighting the school rules won't help her learn to cope with adversity. Instead, it will teach her that you don't think she can adjust to challenging situations.

Instead, tell yourself,

"I'm doing the best thing for my child, whether she understands it or not."

Keep in mind that as a parent, your responsibility is to give your child opportunities that will help her become a self-reliant, well-adjusted, flexible adult. Although she may be disappointed or frustrated now, helping her learn to cope with her feelings will serve her well later on.

Don't tell yourself,

> *"I hate upsetting my child. I'll just let her stay home."*

First, remember that you don't upset your child; only she can control how she feels. Second, giving in to her complaints will teach her that all she has to do is whine and fuss to get her way. Finally, retracting your request won't teach her to cope with doing things she doesn't want to do.

Instead, tell yourself,

> *"I can endure my child's discomfort right now.*
> *She'll eventually adjust to the situation."*

Getting upset won't help you solve the problem; it will only teach your child to get upset when she doesn't get her way. Remember, this too shall pass. Reacting calmly to the situation will help your child do the same.

Don't tell yourself,

> *"I'm ruining her life by insisting that she stay in the*
> *room with the little kids. She'll probably hate me forever."*

Don't exaggerate the problem. Your love for your child isn't conditional; her love for you isn't conditional, either.

Instead, tell yourself,

> *"Being with the little kids isn't that big a deal."*

Putting minor problems in perspective helps you cope with them. When you remain calm and relaxed, you open your mind to creative problem solving.

Talking to Your Child

Don't discount. Don't say,

> *"I don't care if you don't like the little kids' room.*
> *You're stuck there, so just deal with it."*

Your lack of empathy tells your child that she can't expect any support from you. Without your support, her isolation can lead her to feel unwanted and unloved.

Instead, remind her about the rule. Say,

> *"I know you don't like being in the room with the little kids,*
> *but the rule says that you have to stay there for a little while.*
> *Let's think of fun things to do while you're there."*

Empathize with your child's plight while explaining the rule. When she sees that you respect her enough to take her concerns seriously, she'll be motivated to cooperate.

Don't scold. Don't say,

**"Stop your whining about the little kid's room.
I don't want to hear it anymore."**

Dismissing your child's concerns tells her that her feelings aren't important. Although you may not be in the mood to listen to her complaints, putting her down won't solve the problem and will only increase her anger and resentment.

Instead, be proactive. Say,

"Tell me about the fun things that happened in preschool today."

When your child complains about her room assignment, help her focus on the positive aspects of preschool. Doing so tells her that complaining isn't as much fun as thinking about the good things. What a healthy lesson!

Don't bribe. Don't say,

**"If you'll stop complaining about being in the room
with the little kids, I'll buy you a new toy on the way home."**

Bribing your child will teach her that she'll be rewarded if she bottles up her emotions. You want to teach her the opposite lesson: that you're always available when she needs to share her feelings, and that you want her to do so.

Instead, focus on the positives. Say,

"Tell me about what you do with your friends at preschool."

Help your child share good feelings about her room assignment to teach her to look for the positives instead of dwelling on the negatives. Positive feelings have been shown to improve circulation, ease depression, and promote good health.

Don't belittle. Don't say,

**"If you're going to be such a crybaby about it,
you belong with the little kids."**

Ouch! Calling your child names tells her you don't care about her feelings. Take this hurtful, unproductive response out of your repertoire.

Instead, praise cooperative behavior. Say,

**"It's so grown-up of you to go to preschool,
even when you don't like being in the little kids' room."**

Praising your child for coping will encourage her to manage her frustration. She wants to please you and will repeat positive behaviors to get your praise.

Chapter Forty-six

"It's Time to Practice Now."
"No! I Don't Wanna Practice!"

This timeless complaint speaks to the pressure parents put on their children to excel—and the rebellion preschoolers stage when feeling pressured to meet certain expectations. Understand your child's need for stimulation *and* rest, so you avoid overloading him with too many activities. Encourage practice, but don't demand that your child learn to do things that are beyond his developmental level.

Helpful Hints

🖐 Establish a regular practice time so it becomes a routine.

🖐 Make sure your child has plenty of free time to choose his own activities.

Self-Talk

Don't tell yourself,
"My child never wants to practice. He's so lazy."
Don't exaggerate your child's unwillingness to practice. Attributing his reluctance to laziness puts a label on *him* instead of his behavior. He may be tired, he may not care about the lesson, or he may lack motivation, but he's not lazy.

Instead, tell yourself,
"I understand that practice can be dull and boring."
Use empathy to understand how your child feels. Think about tasks that you don't like to do, and appreciate the difficulty you've had overcoming boredom.

Don't tell yourself,

"I'm worried that he won't do well in his recital if he doesn't practice."
Worrying about your child's potential failure won't help him develop good practice habits. Speculating on disaster will only increase your anxiety; it won't help you focus on the task at hand.

Instead, tell yourself,

"It's not the end of the world if my child doesn't want to practice today."
Understanding that your child's resistance is temporary keeps you from believing that you *must* find a way to make him practice.

Don't tell yourself,

"It's not my job to teach him. That's his teacher's job."
Your child's education requires that you and his teacher work together. Abdicating your responsibility does a disservice to your child. Indeed, you are your child's first and most important teacher.

Instead, tell yourself,

"My job is to help my child develop good practice habits."
Motivating your child to practice isn't just about improving his skills; it's about developing his self-discipline and perseverance—skills he'll need throughout his life.

Don't tell yourself,

"I'm tired of fighting with him about practicing. He'll just have to fail and then maybe he'll learn to practice."
Using failure to attempt to motivate your child won't teach him how to persevere to achieve a goal.

Instead, tell yourself,

"I won't give up on him despite his resistance."
Helping your child stick to his goals will not only help him develop necessary skills, it will show him how to persist when challenged. Modeling perseverance yourself will reinforce its importance in your child's mind.

Talking to Your Child

Don't use fear. Don't say,
"You'll never get into a good kindergarten if you don't practice your letters."
Don't use your child's success or failure to determine your self-worth. Using fear to motivate him makes your happiness dependent on his performance. Your child may cooperate, but only to avoid disappointing you.

Instead, compliment your child. Say,
"You're doing so well in your practice today. Doesn't it feel good to work hard and accomplish something?"
Praising your child's effort can help establish a lifelong habit of working hard to reach goals. Remember to praise his *effort*, not the outcome.

Don't use guilt. Don't say,
"I thought you liked playing piano. Why don't you want to practice?"
Asking your child why he doesn't want to do something backs him into a corner and makes him defensive as he tries to explain his behavior.

Instead, offer support. Say,
"Let's practice your scales. I'll sit here with you to keep you company."
Your presence and attention may provide all the motivation your child needs. He'll learn that you value his lessons enough to take the time to sit with him.

Don't compare. Don't say,
"Your brother always practiced without fussing."
Comparing your child to his sibling will likely increase sibling rivalry. Your job is to help your children reach their potential, regardless of their siblings' accomplishments.

Instead, remind him about the rule. Say,
"The clock says it's time to practice. When the timer rings, practice will be over."
Putting the timer in charge removes you from the role of enforcer and lets your child manage himself. In addition, it avoids the comparison to anyone else's practice habits.

SECTION VIII
SLEEPING

There is always a time for
gratitude and new beginnings.
—*J. Robert Moskin*

Chapter Forty-seven

"It's Time to Get Ready for Bed."
"No! I Don't Wanna Go to Bed!"

Getting ready for bed starts to be attractive only when no one is telling you to do so. Maintain a consistent bedtime routine and make sure your preschooler's pj's fit well. Children thrive on predictability and consistency.

Helpful Hints

☟ Make a rule that establishes the time when your child needs to put on her pajamas. Give her a few minutes' advance warning.

☟ Use a timer to govern each step of the bedtime routine.

☟ Engage in quiet, calming activities as bedtime approaches (reading stories, getting a back rub, saying prayers, and so on).

☟ You may want to designate clothing that's worn only for sleeping, so putting it on reminds your child that bedtime is coming soon.

Self-Talk

Don't tell yourself,
"I'm exhausted at night and don't have any patience to enforce bedtime."
Don't let pessimism ruin your ability to overcome fatigue. Thinking is believing. If you tell yourself you can't do it, you won't be able to.

Instead, tell yourself,
"I can handle my child's resistance even when I'm tired."
Affirming your ability to cope will give you the energy you need to gain your child's cooperation. Positive self-talk is contagious.

Don't tell yourself,

"I get so angry when she doesn't do what I tell her to do."
First, demanding your child's cooperation is unrealistic and counterproductive. Second, getting angry blocks your ability to think of reasonable ways to solve the problem, and it models anger as an acceptable reaction to life's frustrations.

Instead, tell yourself,

"I can stay calm when my child doesn't want to get her pajamas on."
Maintain self-control when your child doesn't want to end her day. Doing so will keep your attitude and interactions with her positive. In addition, it will help you solve the problem with an open mind.

Don't tell yourself,

"If I don't have her in bed by eight o'clock, my evening is ruined."
This attitude not only puts tremendous pressure on you and your child, it creates an unrealistic objective. *You* decide whether your evening is "ruined," not your child.

Instead, tell yourself,

**"I understand that my child doesn't
want the excitement of the day to end."**
Appreciating your child's perspective helps you empathize with her desires when they don't match your agenda. This puts you in a much better position to elicit her cooperation.

Talking to Your Child

Don't threaten. Don't say,

"Are you deaf? You'd better get those pj's on before I swat your bottom!"
Threatening to hurt your child teaches her that threatening violence can help people get what they want. You don't want her to use violence, so don't model it for her.

Instead, ask her opinion. Say,

"Tell me what you don't like about getting your pj's on."
Asking your child to share her thoughts teaches her that you care about them and gives her practice at expressing them. After she tells you what she thinks, you can focus on solving the problem instead of nagging and whining about her behavior.

Don't use fear. Don't say,

> *"I've had a bad day, so don't mess with me.*
> *Just get in there and put your pajamas on."*

Don't tell your child that she needs to monitor your mood to avoid confrontation. Remember, events are neutral; they become "good" or "bad" based on what you think about them. You don't have to allow a tough day at the office to contaminate your behavior toward your child.

Instead, remind her about the rule. Say,

> *"I understand that you don't want to get your pj's on,*
> *but the rule says we have to have them on by seven o'clock."*

We all live by rules: traffic rules, school rules, job rules—and bedtime rules. Teach your child that following the rules is a way of life. Deferring to the rule lets you be on your child's side in a dispute.

Don't punish. Don't say,

> *"You don't want to put your pj's on? Okay, then you're in time-out.*
> *You can sit there until you're ready to put your pj's on."*

Using time-out defeats the purpose of getting your child into bed on time. In addition, it teaches her that she can delay bedtime by refusing to put on her pajamas.

Instead, use a timer. Say,

> *"You're getting your clothes off so quickly.*
> *I'm sure you'll beat the timer getting your pj's on."*

Use a timer to set up a competition, and praise your child's progress toward winning the race. Playing the game distracts your child from her rebellion and gets the job done.

Chapter Forty-eight

"It's Time to Take a Nap."
"No! I Don't Wanna Take a Nap!"

A three-year-old's protests against naps are usually the loudest when he's totally exhausted. He may be objecting to the perceived double standard: You're up doing stuff, so why can't he? Let him know that nap time is your quiet time, too. If he knows you're settling down, it may help him do the same.

Helpful Hints

🖐 Establish a nap-time routine and follow it consistently.

🖐 Make rules about nap time or resting time, and let a timer dictate the minimum time for naps or resting.

🖐 Choose quiet activities before nap time so your child can begin to settle down.

Self-Talk

Don't tell yourself,

"I'm too tired to be nice to my child. He'll just have to understand that."
Don't use exhaustion as an excuse for being unkind. Doing so teaches your child the inappropriate lesson that respect for others is conditional.

Instead, tell yourself,

"We're both tired, but that's no excuse for me to get cranky."
This positive message will help you avoid blaming your mood on your fatigue. You're responsible for teaching your child that it's important to behave appropriately whether you're tired or not.

Don't tell yourself,

"When my child doesn't take a nap, the rest of my day is shot."
By predicting disaster, you create a self-fulfilling prophecy and irrationally blame the outcome of your day on your child.

Instead, tell yourself,

> *"My child's refusal to nap doesn't mean my day is ruined."*

You control what you think about your child's refusal to nap. By staying calm when your child resists, you show him how to cope with frustration.

Don't tell yourself,

> *"I can't stand to listen to him cry, so I'll just let him stay up."*

No parent likes to hear a child cry, but allowing him to stay up won't teach him how to deal with adversity.

Instead, tell yourself,

> *"I can handle my child's refusal to sleep,*
> *but he still needs to have quiet time."*

It's possible that your child may not need to nap anymore. Give him the option of having quiet time instead, but make sure he understands that he has to do one or the other.

Don't tell yourself,

> *"I don't care if he doesn't take a nap."*

Giving up on nap time or quiet time teaches your child that his resistance will eventually pay off.

Instead, tell yourself,

> *"Even though he resists taking a nap,*
> *I know it's important for him to have some rest time."*

Recognizing the importance of rest will give you greater resolve to enforce the rule. It'll be good for him—and you.

Talking to Your Child

Don't threaten. Don't say,

> *"Get in there and go to sleep before I spank you."*

Your lack of empathy and threat of physical pain won't help your child feel comfortable and relaxed enough to rest. In addition, he'll learn that if you're bigger and stronger, you can intimidate others to get your way.

Instead, remind him about the rule. Say,
> *"I know you don't want to go to sleep now,*
> *but the rule says you have to rest until the timer rings."*

Remind your child of the rule, and let the timer enforce it. This will help you avoid conflict and stay positive.

Don't use guilt. Don't say,
> *"I'm sick and tired of your whining about quiet time.*
> *Just shut up and get in your room."*

Telling your child that he makes you sick and tired not only tells him that your love is conditional, it models bullying, a behavior you don't want him to imitate.

Instead, make a deal. Say,
> *"When you've had your quiet time, then we can have*
> *your friend come over to play later this afternoon."*

Use Grandma's Rule to focus your child's attention on the future fun after quiet time.

Don't nag. Don't say,
> *"How many times do I have to tell you to take a nap?"*

Nagging won't accomplish what you want (your child's cooperation), but it will produce an unfortunate side effect (teaching *him* to nag).

Instead, be positive. Say,
> *"Isn't it nice that we're both going to have quiet time now?*
> *Then we can have lots of energy for the rest of the day."*

Having a positive attitude and modeling rest time for your child help him see the benefit of following your directions.

Chapter Forty-nine

"It's Time for You to Sleep in a Big Bed."
"No! I Don't Wanna Sleep in a Big Bed!"

You know your two-year-old needs to move out of her crib, but she's not buying any part of the "big girl" adventure. Remind yourself that change is stressful for young children and that she's upset about being taken out of her comfort zone. Talk positively about the transition for at least two weeks prior to the big day, and plan to make several major changes at once to avoid forcing her to adjust to each one separately. For example, have her move to the big bed, rearrange her room, and get new curtains all at the same time. If you think your child would do better with several minor changes implemented gradually, then go that route. You know your child best.

Helpful Hints

✋ Make sure your child can sleep in a big bed without falling out. If necessary, place a temporary guardrail on the bed to protect her. Avoid putting her in an upper bunk bed until she's at least six years old.

✋ Encourage your child to bring a couple of "friends" in bed with her (stuffed animals, dolls, and so on) to help with the transition.

✋ Buy some sheets in her favorite color or with her favorite cartoon character on them to make the change more attractive.

Self-Talk

Don't tell yourself,
"This is going to be a bigger hassle than it's worth, so I'm going to let her stay in the crib."
Expecting a major battle is one way of ensuring it will happen. Delaying the task won't make it go away.

Instead, tell yourself,

> **"I can expect some resistance from my child for big changes, but I can cope with it."**

Affirm your ability to handle your child's protests. Your positive attitude will help you remain calm and patient and will help her do the same.

Don't tell yourself,

> **"Why does it have to be like this? Why can't it be easy?"**

It's normal for toddlers and preschoolers to resist change as they struggle to assert their identity and gain control of their world. The situation *can* be easy, if you think of it as such.

Instead, tell yourself,

> **"I understand that the occasional meltdown is part of growing up, but I need to keep my cool."**

Modeling self-control is an important way to guide your child toward developing better self-control. She'll learn from your example.

Don't tell yourself,

> **"My child is so insecure, she won't be able to handle moving to a big bed."**

When you decide that your child is insecure, you give up on her ability to become confident and handle change.

Instead, tell yourself,

> **"My goal is to help my child learn to cope with change."**

Your child is able to do anything she puts her heart and mind to. Part of learning to cope is developing the confidence to accept change even when it's frightening.

Talking to Your Child

Don't demand. Don't say,

> **"Stop complaining about sleeping in a big bed.
> Your crib is gone, so get in there and go to sleep."**

Your lack of empathy will tell your child that she won't get any emotional support from you. She may cooperate, but only out of fear of your rejection. She won't learn to manage her fear of change.

Instead, remind her about the rule. Say,

> **"The rule says that when you're two years old,
> you get to sleep in a big bed."**

Deferring to the rule makes *it* the villain, so you can remain an ally to your child. Telling her that she "gets" to sleep in a big bed instead of "having" to do so puts a positive spin on the situation and allows her to feel more in control of the decision.

Don't make promises you can't keep. Don't say,

> **"If you'll sleep in your big bed,
> I'll lie down with you until you fall asleep."**

With a "no limit" bribe like this, prepare to spend the next few years putting your child to sleep, because she'll grow to depend on your presence in order to fall asleep.

Instead, use praise. Say,

> **"I'm glad you're being so brave about sleeping in a big bed.
> I'll lie here with you until the timer rings and
> tells me I have to go sleep in my bed."**

Affirming your child's bravery will help her warm up to her new arrangement. Letting the timer dictate how long you can stay will help her adjust to the change.

Don't reverse your decision. Don't say,

> **"I can't stand hearing you cry,
> so I'll get your baby bed back out so you can sleep in it."**

Reversing your decision teaches your child that crying is her ticket to getting her way. It also models a lack of persistence; you're giving in because you're frustrated, not because you've changed your mind.

Instead, reframe the situation. Say,

> **"Your new bed is big enough for me to lie here
> with you while we read books. Isn't that nice?"**

Focusing your child on the benefits of the new bed will help shift her attention away from the old one.

Chapter Fifty

"I Want You to Sleep in Your Own Bed." "No! I Don't Wanna Sleep in My Own Bed!"

You want your child to stay in his own bed, but he wants to crawl in with his sister, his dog—or you. Make a rule about where family members should sleep, so the rule is the enforcer. If you've decided that your child should sleep in his own bed, avoid changing the rule. Don't allow him to sleep with you, even if he's sick or if your spouse is out of town. Being consistent reduces the likelihood that he'll test the rules.

Helpful Hints

☙ Establish bedtime rules and routines so your child knows what to expect.

☙ If you've been cosleeping with your child and have decided he needs to move into his own bed, explain the new rule and enforce it consistently.

Self-Talk

Don't tell yourself,

> *"I can't stand to hear my child cry in the middle of the night, so I'll let him come in with me."*

Nothing rips at a parent's heart more than a crying child. However, if you know your child isn't sick or hurt, avoid changing your rule about sleeping in his own bed. Giving in teaches him that crying will eventually get him what he wants, and that your rules don't really matter.

Instead, tell yourself,

> *"I don't like to hear my child cry, but I can handle it while he adjusts to sleeping in his own bed."*

Keeping your long-term goal in mind will help you overcome your child's short-term lack of cooperation. Staying calm will help you cope with his protests.

Don't tell yourself,

> *"Everyone will think I'm crazy for letting my child sleep with me."*

Worrying about others' opinions gives them power over your decision making. You should make decisions that are best for your family, not ones that cater to others' opinions.

Instead, tell yourself,

> *"I don't care what others think of my sleeping arrangements. I have to do what I think is best."*

Base your parenting decisions on *your* values and beliefs, not someone else's.

Don't tell yourself,

> *"I hate my ex for letting my child sleep in his bed at his house."*

Hating your ex for having different rules is a waste of energy. Such thoughts will only increase the tension between the two of you and may potentially damage your child's relationship with his other parent. The only space you control is your own.

Instead, tell yourself,

> *"I need to accept that my ex has different rules at his house."*

Accepting that others have different rules will help prevent a war and will avoid making your child divide his loyalty to his parents.

Talking to Your Child

Don't threaten. Don't say,

> *"Stop that crying or I'll give you something to cry about!"*

Threatening your child with violence when he's upset shuts down his ability to cope and increases his anger and resentment.

Instead, remind him about the rule. Say,

> *"I know you want to sleep in my bed, but the rule says that we all sleep in our own beds."*

Letting the rule determine where everybody sleeps prevents conflict between you and your child and teaches him that it's important to follow rules.

Don't bribe. Don't say,

> *"If you sleep in your own bed, I'll buy you that new toy you wanted."*

Don't be tempted to bribe your child into submission. Bribing teaches your child that your agenda isn't important enough for him to follow without a payoff.

Instead, make a deal. Say,

> *"When you stay in your bed at night,*
> *then we can enjoy breakfast together in the morning."*

Grandma's Rule lets you negotiate something your child wants for something you want. This important lesson models a way to meet everyone's agenda.

Don't give in. Don't say,

> *"Okay, you've been crying long enough.*
> *You can come into bed with me."*

Changing your rule because your child is crying is a dangerous habit for both you and your child. Decide ahead of time when you'll need to respond. If you're hearing a whining cry, you may decide to leave him alone. If you're hearing a distressed cry, you may decide to go check on him.

Instead, shift the focus. Say,

> *"I know you feel lonesome sleeping in your room by yourself,*
> *but you have your teddy bear with you to keep you company.*
> *You can talk to him."*

Help your child focus on how he can manage by himself. Show him that you understand his need for companionship, but that he has the courage to handle sleeping on his own.

Don't blame. Don't say,

> *"Just because your mother lets you sleep in her*
> *bed doesn't mean you can sleep in here with me."*

Blaming the other parent for your child's unwillingness to sleep in his own bed won't teach him to take responsibility for his choices and won't help him learn to sleep alone.

Instead, teach flexibility. Say,

> *"I know you get to sleep in Mommy's bed when you're at*
> *her house, but here you need to sleep in your own bed."*

Help your child learn that different places have different rules. This teaches him to adapt to different environments and makes you his ally, not his enemy.

SECTION IX
GROWING UP

These are the magic years…
and therefore magic moments.

—*Anonymous*

Chapter Fifty-one

"The Baby Is Going to Have Your Room." "No! I Don't Want the Baby to Have My Room!"

Someone's coming over, taking over your space, and never leaving—someone you don't even know. That's how your two-year-old feels when you tell her she has to move out of her room because the baby will be moving in. To ease the transition, enlist your older child's help as you prepare her new room. If possible, choose furniture, paint the walls, decorate, and complete other preparations well in advance of the baby's arrival.

Helpful Hints

✋ Consider your child's personality to help gauge her reaction to the move. Does she "go with the flow" or does she have difficulty being flexible? This information will let you modify your approach when helping her cope with the change.

✋ Talk about the arrival of the new baby positively so your child will look upon the new family member as a friend, not an enemy!

Self-Talk

Don't tell yourself,
"I don't want to see my child upset, so we'll just leave things as they are."
Although avoiding the change may be tempting, it won't create the space needed for the baby and won't teach your child to cope with change. She needs to experience change to learn to cope with it.

Instead, tell yourself,
"If I cope well with change, then my child will learn to cope well, too."
Your enthusiasm sends your child the message that moving to a new room is an exciting event. Your example teaches her to embrace a change as a challenge rather than fear it as a threat.

Don't tell yourself,

> **"I'm disgusted that she doesn't appreciate all**
> **the hard work we've put into her new room."**

Loving unconditionally means giving without expecting anything in return. Feeling disgusted because your child doesn't react positively to change teaches her that you only love her when she meets your approval.

Instead, tell yourself,

> **"I can understand my child's reluctance to give up her room."**

Your toddler or preschooler is egocentric and unconcerned with what you've done to the new room. She's struggling with feeling displaced. Your positive attitude toward her struggle will help her feel supported and loved as she deals with the change.

Don't tell yourself,

> **"What's wrong with my child?**
> **She should be excited about moving into a new room."**

Believing that there's something "wrong" with your child or that she should behave in one way or another suggests that you control her thoughts, feelings, and behaviors. Wrong! All you can control is your reaction to them.

Instead, tell yourself,

> **"I've had problems adjusting to change,**
> **so I can understand my child's distress."**

Empathizing with your child makes her feel like you're on the same team, which helps her want to cooperate and follow your directions.

Talking to Your Child

Don't be disrespectful. Don't say,

> **"I don't care if you want to stay in your old room.**
> **You'll just have to get used to the new one."**

Your lack of empathy tells your child that you're her enemy in this crisis. No one wants to cooperate with the enemy.

Instead, redirect your child's attention. Say,

> **"I understand that you don't want to leave this room, but your**
> **new room is so nice. Let's look at all the good things about it."**

Talking about her new room's benefits models viewing change with a positive attitude.

Don't bribe. Don't say,

> *"If you let the baby have your room,*
> *I'll buy you that new headband you've been wanting."*

As a parent, it's your job to establish rules; your preschooler's job is to test them. When you offer a bribe, you tell your child that your rule is meaningless; she doesn't need to follow it until she gets something for doing so. Your child needs to learn to do a task because it's the rule, not because she'll get a prize for doing it.

Instead, make a deal. Say,

> *"You've been asking to have your friend sleep over,*
> *so when you've moved into your new room, you can invite her.*
> *You can show her how nice your new room is."*

Grandma's Rule lets your child feel that she has some control over her life, which helps her at a time when she's feeling displaced.

Don't use putdowns. Don't say,

> *"I'm not going to put up with your nonsense. Stop being such a baby."*

Being a baby is the role your two-year-old has had all her life, so it's normal for her to resist when you fault her for playing it. In addition, she won't want to follow directions when you tell her that her heartfelt protests are nonsense.

Instead, be proactive. Say,

> *"I need your help in getting your old room ready for the baby.*
> *You'll know how to make the baby feel good in this*
> *room because you liked it so well."*

Make your child part of the welcoming committee for the new baby. This will give her an important role in the transition and will help her focus on the positive ways she can relate to her new sibling, her new identity, and her new quarters.

Don't beg. Don't say,

> *"Please cooperate so we can use your room for the baby."*

Begging your child to cooperate teaches her to beg to get her way. Your goal is to motivate her to follow your directions by pointing out how she'll benefit.

Instead, include your child. Say,

**"Let's go to the shopping center to look
at ways to decorate your new room."**

Engaging your child in the plans and asking for her input validates her ownership of her new space and tells her that her ideas are important.

Don't tease. Don't say,

**"Why are you afraid to move?
Do you think there's a boogieman in your new room?"**

Teasing your child will teach her that you don't care about her feelings, and it will show her how to tease others to get what she wants.

Instead, use praise. Say,

**"You're so brave and strong.
I know you'll be okay in your new room."**

Helping your child focus on her strengths teaches her to appreciate her ability to handle change. She'll be happy to accept change when you support her ability to do so. We all want this kind of validation.

Chapter Fifty-two

"You're Going to Have a Babysitter Tonight." *"No! I Don't Wanna Babysitter!"*

Your four-year-old wants you around *all* the time and can't understand why you'd ever want to leave him, whether you've been together all day or not. You can see why he'd fuss when you tell him you're going out and he's going to be left behind. To make your time apart pleasant and enjoyable, find sitters who share your child's interests and who can relate to him on his developmental level. Remember to make goodbyes short and sweet so your child doesn't make a habit of clinging to you while you're leaving.

Helpful Hints

- ✋ Plan a regular night out so your child can get accustomed to having a sitter.

- ✋ Prepare your child well ahead of time when you're planning an evening out. Give positive reminders throughout the day so he won't be surprised when the sitter arrives and you leave.

- ✋ Many sitters become "special friends" because they love to play with your child and help him learn new skills safely. Referring to them as "special friends" instead of sitters helps strengthen your child's bond with them and helps him cope when separated from you.

Self-Talk

Don't tell yourself,
> *"It upsets me so much to hear my child cry when we leave."*

If you tell yourself you're going to get upset, you will. Only *you* control whether or not you get upset when your child cries. Getting upset prevents you from helping him cope with the separation.

Instead, tell yourself,
> *"I know my child doesn't like us to leave, but I know he'll get over it."*

Telling yourself that your child's distress is temporary will help you cope with the fuss, and staying calm will help him calm down.

Don't tell yourself,

"I guess we'll just have to wait till he's older to go out."

Changing your plans because your child gets upset won't teach him to cope when he doesn't get his way. Instead, it will teach him that he can control your decisions by fussing.

Instead, tell yourself,

"My job is to help my child learn to cope with change."

Affirming your long-term goal lets you deal more effectively with your child's struggle to separate from you.

Don't tell yourself,

"I feel so guilty about leaving him when he's upset, especially when he's been in daycare all day."

Guilt comes from believing you've doing something wrong by having him in daycare all day.

Instead, tell yourself,

"I'm glad my child is getting a chance to tolerate frustration."

You're responsible for finding a competent sitter, writing down relevant phone numbers, providing child-care instructions, and reassuring your child that you'll be home soon. Doing so will give you the rest you need and will let your child practice being away from you.

Talking to Your Child

Don't give in. Don't say,

"Okay. If you don't want us to go out, we won't."

Giving in to your child's protests won't let him practice being separated from you. He needs to learn to cope with separation in order to become independent and self-sufficient.

Instead, empathize. Say,

"I'm sorry you don't want us to go, but Mommy and Daddy are going out to dinner. We'll come in and kiss you when we get home."

Empathize with your child while being firm about leaving. Doing so teaches him that you care about his feelings, and reassures him that he'll be okay while you're gone.

Don't belittle. Don't say,
> *"What's the matter with you? I thought you liked your sitter!"*

Don't suggest there's something wrong with your child because he doesn't want a sitter. This tells him that his feelings are unacceptable and that you'll never tolerate his disagreeing with you.

Instead, be positive. Say,
> *"Your special friend, Laurie, is coming.*
> *You like her, and you always have so much fun together."*

Help your child look beyond his concern about separating from you toward the fun he'll have with his "special friend."

Don't threaten. Don't say,
> *"Since you make such a fuss whenever we leave,*
> *we're going to sneak out so you won't know."*

Never try this trick! Telling your child that you won't inform him when you leave violates his trust in you and increases his anxiety about your leaving. It also teaches him that it's okay for *him* to sneak out and not tell you.

Instead, offer a choice. Say,
> *"We're going out on Friday night.*
> *What special friend do you want to come over and stay with you?"*

Motivate your child to cooperate by letting him help select who'll stay with him while you're gone. He'll feel important and validated because you value his opinion.

Don't shame. Don't say,
> *"I'm ashamed of you for making such a fuss in front of the sitter."*

Telling your child his behavior is shameful will only make separation harder for him. He'll feel that he's disappointed you and that he isn't capable of doing what you've asked.

Instead, use praise. Say,
> *"We're going out this evening,*
> *and a new sitter is coming to stay with you until we get back.*
> *You're brave and strong and can handle our being away for a while."*

Tell your child about your plans early in the day, and affirm his ability to handle separation.

Chapter Fifty-three

"I'd Like You to Help Me, Please."
"No! I Don't Wanna Help!"

You repeatedly ask your three-year-old to bring you a diaper for her baby brother. The more she ignores you, the angrier you get. Instead of whining about it or nagging her, use the opportunity to understand her point of view. Is she jealous of the baby? Is she unable to hear you? Does she understand what you're asking? Is she busy with her own activities? Understanding her position will help you choose how to teach her to be supportive and cooperative, two skills that will help her feel good about herself and help others feel good about her.

Helpful Hints

🖐 Model empathy, caring, and helpfulness so your child will appreciate the importance of these behaviors.

🖐 Praise *any* helpfulness your child offers, to encourage her to repeat the behavior.

🖐 Consider what your older child is doing before asking her for help. Perhaps she needs time to finish her project, for example, before helping you.

Self-Talk

Don't tell yourself,

"She never wants to help. Where did I go wrong?"

Don't exaggerate the situation by using words like *never*, and avoid blaming yourself for the problem. Doing so creates strong negative emotions that block your ability to solve the problem.

Instead, tell yourself,

"It's no big deal that she doesn't want to help. I can handle that."

Keeping the problem in perspective will help you focus on possible solutions. Your child's resistance may frustrate and irritate you, but telling yourself you can handle it is the first step toward doing so.

Don't tell yourself,

"She's always been a selfish child."

Labeling your child as selfish makes the problem permanent, which makes you feel helpless in finding a solution.

Instead, tell yourself,

"My job is to help my child learn to be a kind, caring person."

Focus on the long-term goal to help you stay on track as you teach your child to cooperate.

Don't tell yourself,

"She makes me so mad when I ask her for help and she ignores me."

Don't get angry because your child won't respond to your request. This will only make it more difficult to solve the problem.

Instead, tell yourself,

"I don't need to feel angry because she doesn't want to help."

You control your anger. Choose to look at the situation as an opportunity to teach your child to be helpful, rather than as another frustrating moment in a long line of frustrating moments.

Talking to Your Child

Don't threaten. Don't say,

"Don't you ignore me, young lady!
Get in here and help me or you'll be in time-out!"

Don't try to motivate your child by demanding compliance. Doing so won't help her develop empathy and caring, the true motivation for helping someone else.

Instead, use praise. Say,

"I really need your help, and you're such a good helper."

Telling your child that you need her help will show her that she's a valued member of the family.

Don't use guilt. Don't say,

"What's the matter with you? I do everything for you all day long,
and you won't lift a finger to help me!"

Ouch! This response diminishes your child's self-worth and ability to accept making mistakes. It also damages your relationship with her. Suggesting that she's flawed sends the erroneous message that her behavior defines who she is.

Instead, invite feedback. Say,

> *"Tell me what you're thinking when*
> *I ask you to get a diaper for your baby brother."*

Your respectful request will give you insight into your child's behavior and help you determine a course of action. It will also help your child develop the healthy habit of expressing herself.

Don't get angry. Don't say,

> *"You make me so mad when you ignore me.*
> *Now get in here and help me!"*

Telling your child that she causes your anger diminishes her ability to empathize and makes her believe she has tremendous power over your emotions—a scary prospect for her. In reality, *you* are the only one who controls your feelings.

Instead, make a deal. Say,

> *"When you've gotten the diaper for me,*
> *then we can read that book you've been asking me to read to you."*

Think about how you can help your child meet her agenda, and use that to motivate her to cooperate. This use of Grandma's Rule shows her that when she's done what you've asked, then you can help her do what she wants.

Don't create fear. Don't say,

> *"I guess I'll have to go out and find another*
> *little girl who'll help me with your brother."*

Don't try to motivate your child through fear! Suggesting that you'll abandon her won't teach her to want to help. It will, however, teach her that your love is conditional—that it comes and goes depending on her behavior. She may end up cooperating, but only to try to keep your love, not because she empathizes with you or her sibling. She'll also learn the dangerous and erroneous lesson that she is what she does.

Instead, use praise. Say,

> *"Thanks so much for your help.*
> *I don't know what I'd do without my helper."*

Telling your child that you depend on her will motivate her to want to cooperate. To a child, love is spelled p-r-a-i-s-e.

Chapter Fifty-four

"You're in Time-Out."
"No! I Don't Wanna Be in Time-Out!"

Time-out effectively removes your child from a frustrating situation and helps him calm down. When he resists staying in time-out, your job is to gently but firmly return him to his time-out area. His refusal to cooperate reinforces his need for a brief separation. It's important that you remain calm and loving when taking your child to time-out; don't disrespectfully banish him from the play area. When you stay calm, he'll be more likely to cooperate.

Helpful Hints

☙ Monitor your child during play time so you can intervene before his frustration gets out of hand.

☙ Use time-out to let your child calm down and to reduce the risk of him hurting someone or himself.

☙ Use time-out as a positive consequence that builds self-control, rather than as a punishment for inappropriate behavior.

☙ Use time-out for inappropriate social behavior (hitting, biting, pushing, shoving, grabbing, name-calling) to show your child that respecting people is extremely important.

Self-Talk

Don't tell yourself,
"I'm a terrible parent. If I could control my child, he wouldn't behave so badly and have to go to time-out."
First, you can't control your child's behavior; you can only guide it. Second, avoid blaming yourself for your child's choices or telling yourself that putting him in time-out is bad. When you blame yourself, your guilt prevents you from effectively managing the situation.

Instead, tell yourself,
> *"I'm going to use time-out to help my child calm down."*

Use time-out to help your child calm down rather than to humiliate or inflict pain on him. Instead of feeling guilty about putting him in time-out, remind yourself that he's learning to regroup and refocus on appropriate behavior.

Don't tell yourself,
> *"My child makes me so mad when he embarrasses me in front of my friends."*

Don't blame your child for your anger and embarrassment. Doing so will make you want to punish him rather than teach him to choose self-calming and cooperative behavior.

Instead, tell yourself,
> *"Keeping myself calm while putting my child in time-out will help him calm down."*

Remaining calm teaches your child that self-control is an effective way to handle difficult situations.

Talking to Your Child

Don't label. Don't say,
> *"If you weren't such a bad kid, you wouldn't have to go to time-out."*

Telling your child that he's bad will create a self-fulfilling prophecy. Expect your child to live *up*, rather than *down*, to your expectations.

Instead, remind him about the rule. Say,
> *"I understand that you don't want to go to time-out, but the rule says that because you chose to hit, you also chose to stop playing for a while."*

Show your child that his choices result in predictable consequences.

Don't rescue. Don't say,
> *"Okay, I know you're sorry. You don't have to stay in time-out."*

Don't rescue your child from accepting responsibility for his actions, even though you think doing so will solve the problem. This teaches him that all he has to do is say he's sorry to avoid time-out.

Instead, make a deal. Say,

> **"When you've stayed in time-out until the timer rings,**
> **then you may come back to play."**

Grandma's Rule teaches your child to delay gratification and demonstrates your respect for his need to rejoin the fun.

Don't use guilt. Don't say,

> **"If you'd behave like you're supposed to,**
> **you wouldn't have to go to time-out."**

Avoid guilt-tripping your child to motivate him to cooperate. Doing so doesn't show him the benefits of choosing appropriate behavior when he's frustrated.

Instead, stay positive. Say,

> **"Time-out helps us calm down. When we're calm,**
> **we can make better choices and have more fun."**

Point out the benefits of getting away from the action for a while. This helps your child learn the valuable lesson of removing himself from a tense situation when he gets upset.

Don't threaten. Don't say,

> **"I told you to go to time-out! Now get back in there or I'll spank you!"**

Threatening physical pain to gain your child's cooperation teaches him that threatening is an acceptable way to control people's behavior. Getting angry prevents you from teaching him how to behave appropriately and gives his behavior negative attention.

Instead, empathize. Say,

> **"I'm sorry you chose not to stay in time-out.**
> **Now you'll have to start time-out all over again."**

Telling your child you're sorry models empathy for him, but returning him to time-out tells him that he still needs to follow the rule.

Chapter Fifty-five

"Let's Leave Your Blanket at Home."
"No! I Wanna Bring My Blanket!"

Your three-year-old drags her favorite blanket (or pacifier) everywhere. You fear she'll take it to kindergarten if you don't get her weaned from it. To help your child wean herself from comfort items, establish boundaries for their use and help her find other ways to comfort herself. Finding ways to compromise will meet both your agendas and help you feel good about this transition.

Helpful Hints

✋ Provide a warm, nurturing environment so your child feels safe giving up comfort items.

✋ Make rules about where and when your child can use blankets, pacifiers, stuffed animals, and other comfort items.

✋ Use birthdays as transition times to give up comfort items. For example, say, "Now that you're five years old, let's practice leaving Teddy at home while you go to kindergarten."

✋ Restrict pacifier use to bedtime only, after consulting with your dentist to ensure that using a pacifier won't damage the alignment of your child's teeth or jaw.

Self-Talk

Don't tell yourself,
"I can't stand seeing my child with that blanket in her arms all the time."
Telling yourself that you can't stand something prevents you from developing ways of coping with it. Negative emotions block your capacity to be creative.

Instead, tell yourself,

"I can live with her needing her blanket until she's ready to give it up."
This "no big deal" attitude tells your child that you respect her need to let go gradually. No one likes to be forced to do something.

Don't tell yourself,

"If I don't take her blanket away from her now, she'll be using it until she graduates from high school."
Exaggerating the problem may make you exert undue pressure on your child to break the habit. If she isn't ready, this will only increase her resistance as she tries to maintain control of her world.

Instead, tell yourself,

"My goal is to help my child develop new ways of comforting herself."
You want to encourage your child to develop other self-comforting techniques, such as drawing pictures, doing a favorite activity, thinking of pleasant events, or looking at books. Remembering this goal will prevent you from letting the immediate problem discourage you.

Don't tell yourself,

"I need to break my child's habit so people will stop looking at me as if I'm a bad parent."
Don't base your parenting decisions on what you think others think about you.

Instead, tell yourself,

"It doesn't matter what people think about my child's pacifier use. She'll give it up when she's ready."
Worrying is a waste of time and energy and can't change what you don't control (others' opinions).

Talking to Your Child

Don't threaten. Don't say,

"If you don't take that binky out of your mouth right now, I'll throw it away."
Never bully your child! Threatening to get rid of her binky is a cruel punishment for a crime she didn't commit. Rather than helping her

cope, bullying will only increase her insecurity and decrease her motivation to give up her binky.

Instead, use a timer. Say,
> *"You may suck on your binky until the timer rings.*
> *Then we have to put it away until tomorrow."*

Using a timer is a nonthreatening way to help you and your child find a healthy compromise, which will increase her motivation to give up her binky.

Don't belittle. Don't say,
> *"What's the matter with you?*
> *Can't you go anywhere without that stupid blanket?"*

Telling your child there's something's the matter with her may lead her to believe that loving her blankie is wrong. In fact, using a special toy or blanket to self-soothe is normal for preschoolers. You may have fond memories of your own special lovie that never left your side when you were her age.

Instead, set limits. Say,
> *"I know you want to take your blankie to the library with us,*
> *but the rule says you can use it only at home."*

Setting boundaries for using comfort items can help your child begin weaning herself from them.

Don't bribe. Don't say,
> *"If you give up your binky, I'll buy you some sparkle paints."*

Bribing your child won't help her give up her lovie. Offering a reward will only distract her from learning to cope with change.

Instead, remind her about the rule. Say,
> *"Remember, the rule says your binky is only for bedtime. I think you*
> *can manage without it until then. Let's find something fun to do."*

Restricting comfort items to certain times and refocusing your child's attention on other activities lets her gradually give up the habit. The key to gaining her cooperation is to make her feel supported and loved.

Don't use putdowns. Don't say,

> *"You look and sound stupid when you have that thing in your mouth. Now take it out so I can understand you."*

Calling your child "stupid" will only increase her need for her binky. Name-calling will also teach her to use that tactic on others when she's frustrated.

Instead, empathize. Say,

> *"I'm sorry. I know you like your binky, but it's important to take it out so people can understand what you're saying."*

Gently explain the problem so your child understands the practical need for removing her pacifier. Let her know that you appreciate how much she loves her binky.

Chapter Fifty-six

"Let's Visit Grandma in the Nursing Home." "No! I Don't Wanna Go See Grandma!"

When it comes to asking your five-year-old to visit an elderly relative, his cooperation may take on added significance in your mind. Remember that he's oblivious to your expectation that visiting Grandma will be meaningful to both you and her. Take the opportunity to share your feelings with him so he'll learn that prioritizing family is a lifelong commitment.

Helpful Hints

🖐 Model kindness, empathy, and caring for grandparents and other older members of your community.

🖐 Avoid complaining about having to visit elderly friends and relatives or about how bad conditions are in the nursing home.

Self-Talk

Don't tell yourself,
"My mother will hate me if I don't bring my son to visit her in the nursing home."
Don't assume your child's resistance will make someone angry at you. Doing so will needlessly pressure you to force him to cooperate.

Instead, tell yourself,
"Just because my child doesn't want to go doesn't mean he's rude."
Recognize that your child's reluctance may result from various factors including anxiety over how Grandma looks, her forgetfulness, or her unpredictable behavior.

Don't tell yourself,
"Where did I go wrong? My child doesn't care about his grandma."
Don't assume that your child is uncaring and that his lack of empathy is your fault. These thoughts will only upset you. Remember, you don't control your child's feelings; he does.

Instead, tell yourself,

"My goal is to help my child develop empathy and compassion."

Your task is to nurture your child's natural empathy through repeated opportunities. Keep this long-term goal in mind to help you cope when he refuses to cooperate.

Don't tell yourself,

"I feel so guilty when my child doesn't want to visit his grandpa."

Feeling guilty implies that you've done something wrong. You aren't to blame for your child's reluctance, and neither is he. You're entitled to your feelings, and he's entitled to his.

Instead, tell yourself,

"I can understand my child's resistance because I don't always want to go myself."

Empathizing with your child will help you find ways to encourage his cooperation. Remember the golden rule: Treat your child as you would want him to treat you.

Talking to Your Child

Don't use guilt. Don't say,

*"What do you mean you don't want to go?
Don't you care about Grandma?"*

Using guilt to motivate your child won't help him develop his abilities to empathize and care for others. Instead, it implies that he's wrong to have certain feelings.

Instead, empathize. Say,

*"I understand you don't want to visit Grandma,
but she loves to see you. I know she'd love for you to visit."*

Helping your child think about how others feel will elicit his natural empathy. Give him time to think about how good it feels to make others happy.

Don't shame. Don't say,

"Grandma will be really mad at you if you don't come."

Don't tell your child that his reluctance will anger Grandma. Doing so will diminish his ability to empathize with her. He'll resent the fact that expressing his true feelings will make someone angry.

Instead, invite feedback. Say,

"Please tell me your reasons for not wanting to go. Help me understand."

Eliciting your child's thoughts will give you important information that may help solve the problem. Maybe he's resisting because the sights, sounds, and smells of the nursing home upset him. If so, ask him to bring Grandma flowers, lotion, or one of his drawings to help sweeten the surroundings.

Don't bribe. Don't say,

**"If you go with me to the nursing home,
then I'll buy you some pizza on the way home."**

Bribing your child will teach him to expect a reward when he does what you've asked. This doesn't teach him the important lesson that caring for others is its own reward.

Instead, make a deal. Say,

**"When we've visited Grandma,
then we can stop at the park on the way home."**

Grandma's Rule teaches your child to meet his responsibilities before fulfilling his desires—a lesson that will help him prioritize his duties as he gets older. It also tells him how he can have control over his life—a goal he's had since birth.

Don't use anger. Don't say,

**"I'm sick and tired of your not wanting to visit Grandma.
Now get in the car!"**

Getting angry will make your child even more fearful and apprehensive. Making your love conditional will tell him he must obey your commands in order to be cared for—a frightening prospect for him.

Instead, offer benefits. Say,

**"Let's bring Grandma the drawing you made this morning.
She'll love to see it, and you'll enjoy showing it to her."**

Focusing your child's attention on making Grandma happy will help draw out his natural empathy. Pointing out how Grandma admires his artwork will strengthen the bond between them.

Chapter Fifty-seven

"Please Walk by Yourself."
"No! I Want You to Carry Me!"

Nothing beats being carried in the arms of a loving parent. Your two-year-old knows this and wants to prolong the treat you've taught her to cherish. Oblige her desire, whenever possible. However, when it's not possible to carry your child, remember that you can help her walk by herself without sacrificing your touch and tenderness.

Helpful Hints

- Make rules about when and how long you can carry your child during an outing.
- Praise your child's ability to walk.
- Remember that your child's legs are shorter than yours and can't cover as much ground as quickly.
- Gradually increase your child's tolerance for walking. Start with short trips around the neighborhood, then begin to lengthen your excursions as her stamina increases.
- Limit stroller use so your child can learn to enjoy walking and get the needed exercise.

Self-Talk

Don't tell yourself,
"I'm exhausted, but she wants me to carry her. I can't disappoint her."
Telling yourself you're exhausted prevents you from finding the strength to manage the situation. Once you've made up your mind you can't do something, your behavior will follow suit.

Instead, tell yourself,

"I can handle my child's disappointment when I can't carry her."

Keep your child's disappointment in perspective; she's entitled to her feelings, and you're entitled to yours. Remind yourself that she won't always get her way, and that she needs practice in coping with disappointment.

Don't tell yourself,

"My child is so lazy."

Labeling your child as lazy makes the problem unchangeable. The truth is that some day she'll be too big for you to carry and will want to walk by herself.

Instead, tell yourself,

"Getting mad at her won't help."

Recognize that *you* control your anger and that your anger isn't good for you or your relationship with your child. Taking responsibility for solving a problem will help you feel hopeful and encouraged.

Don't tell yourself,

"I should carry her."

Telling yourself you "should" do something suggests that there's only one right way to handle the situation. Remind yourself that you're trying to take care of yourself *and* help your child become strong and independent.

Instead, tell yourself,

"I understand my child's desire to be carried."

Empathizing with your child's needs lets you find kind and considerate ways of helping her cope with disappointment.

Talking to Your Child

Don't belittle. Don't say,

"Why can't you walk by yourself?
Do you want to grow up to be fat and lazy?"

Suggesting that your child will become fat and lazy doesn't show her how to cope with her need to be carried, and it may become a self-fulfilling prophecy.

Instead, offer an alternative. Say,
> *"I wish I could carry you, but my hands are full.*
> *When we get home, you can sit on my lap while we read a book."*

Offering your child another option tells her that you value her desire to snuggle and that you want to work with her to find the best way to do that. What teamwork she'll be learning!

Don't bribe. Don't say,
> *"If you'll walk by yourself, I'll stop and buy you some ice cream."*

Bribing your child with food tells her that you should reward her for doing what you ask. It also associates food with your approval—a dangerous strategy that can result in eating disorders and childhood obesity.

Instead, make a deal. Say,
> *"I'm sorry I can't carry you right now,*
> *but we can hold hands while we shop."*

Offering your child an attractive compromise demonstrates sensitivity to her needs without sacrificing your own.

Don't use guilt. Don't say,
> *"Don't you know I'm exhausted?*
> *You only think about yourself. Now just do your own walking."*

Guilt-tripping won't motivate your child to walk so she can become more independent. Instead, it will teach her to comply only because her refusal may hurt you. You don't want her to be afraid to tell you how she feels.

Instead, use positive feedback. Say,
> *"You're walking so well by yourself.*
> *I know you can hold out a little longer."*

Praising your child motivates her to keep going. Her pride in her accomplishment will increase her desire to walk on her own.

Chapter Fifty-eight

"Please Take Your Thumb Out of Your Mouth." "No! I Wanna Suck My Thumb!"

Many a war has been fought between parents and preschoolers over thumb sucking. The American Academy of Pediatric Dentistry states that most children stop thumb sucking on their own between the ages of two and four, and that thumb sucking becomes a concern only when permanent front teeth start erupting around age five. You may want to encourage your child to keep his thumb out of his mouth to avoid sore thumbs, infections, calluses, and so on. On the other hand, appreciate the fact that he finds thumb sucking an easy and convenient way to comfort himself.

Helpful Hints

💜 Take your child to the dentist regularly to assess any damage thumb sucking might be causing.

💜 Enlist your child's dentist to work with you and your child to encourage him to keep his thumb out of his mouth.

Self-Talk

Don't tell yourself,
   "I get so worried when I see my child sucking his thumb."
Getting upset and anticipating calamity prevent you from thinking creatively about solutions.

Instead, tell yourself,
   "I won't worry about my child's thumb sucking, but I will work to find a solution."
Refusing to worry lets you think of ways to help your child keep his thumb out of his mouth. Positive thoughts are also better for your health.

Don't tell yourself,

"What will my mother say if my child keeps sucking his thumb?"

Worrying about others' opinions pressures you to please *them*, which increases the risk of your pressuring your child to stop the behavior. Focusing on other's opinions diverts your attention from the task at hand.

Instead, tell yourself,

"My job is to do what's best for my child."

Remember that your role as a teaching parent is to motivate your child to take his thumb out of his mouth.

Don't tell yourself,

"I should have made my child stop sucking his thumb a long time ago."

Blaming yourself won't help your child learn to keep his thumb out of his mouth, but it will diminish your ability to find solutions. Your mind closes up when you think negatively.

Instead, tell yourself,

"If I stay calm, I have a better chance of helping my child deal with this problem."

Keeping yourself calm lets you think rationally and work toward a solution. It also helps your body language stay open and loving, which encourages your child to cooperate.

Talking to Your Child

Don't threaten. Don't say,

"Get that thumb out of your mouth or I'll put hot sauce on it!"

Threatening to put hot sauce (or soap or pepper) on your child's thumb teaches him that you're willing to inflict pain to force him to cooperate.

Instead, empathize. Say,

"I know it's hard to keep your thumb out of your mouth. Let's find other things that are good for you to do that will keep your hands busy."

Let your child know that you understand how hard it is for him to keep his thumb out of his mouth. Doing so helps him trust what you say. When he feels you're in his corner, he'll be more inclined to cooperate.

Don't bribe. Don't say,

"If you keep your thumb out of your mouth, I'll buy you a new bike."

Promising to give your child a big-ticket item if he does what you ask teaches him to hold out for that promise whenever you request something.

Instead, practice alternative behaviors. Say,

"Let's practice sitting on your hands while you watch TV.
That way you can't put your thumb in your mouth.
Good job sitting on your hands."

Teaching your child preventive behaviors will help him reach the goal you've established. In addition, praising his cooperation will encourage him to repeat the behavior.

Don't discount. Don't say,

"I don't care what your father says when you're at his house.
I'm telling you to get that thumb out of your mouth."

Discounting the other parent teaches your child to divide and conquer in order to get what he wants. Present a united front that has your child's best interests in mind.

Instead, remind him about the goal. Say,

"Keeping your thumb out of your mouth helps you
take care of your new permanent teeth."

Remind your child of the goal: taking care of his teeth. Keep your tone positive so your child focuses on what to do instead of what not to do.

Chapter Fifty-nine

"It's Time to Go Potty."
"No! I Don't Wanna Go Potty!"

The reasons for this protest are as varied as children themselves: not wanting to interrupt their play, being afraid to use toilets in strange places, not feeling the need to go, and so on. Ask your three-year-old to tell you what she's thinking when she resists using the potty, so you can make the experience as easy and comfortable as possible at home or away.

Helpful Hints

☝ Don't constantly ask your child if she has to go potty. She may learn to depend on your asking and avoid initiating toileting herself.

☝ Encourage your child to use the potty before you begin long car trips or other excursions.

☝ Avoid complaining about making a potty stop. Your attitude is contagious.

Self-Talk

Don't tell yourself,
> *"It makes me nuts when she won't go potty when I ask her to—and then she has an accident."*

Telling yourself that your child's behavior makes you crazy puts her in charge of your feelings. *You* choose how you feel in any situation.

Instead, tell yourself,
> *"At this age, not wanting to go potty is normal."*

Take your child's resistance in stride. Keep calm so you can help her learn how to take care of her potty needs.

Don't tell yourself,
> *"What's the matter with my child? Other people's children know how to go potty when they have to."*

It's tempting to think that your child will never measure up to other children when she doesn't want to do what you ask. It's best to avoid comparing your child to other children and making assumptions about what others can do.

Instead, tell yourself,

> *"I don't care if many children stop having accidents at her age.*
> *I know there's nothing wrong with my child."*

When you don't compare your child to others, you can support her and her unique circumstances. Having confidence in your decisions is the best way to help your child.

Don't tell yourself,

> *"I'm sick and tired of my child's refusal to go potty*
> *when she needs to. I'm just going to put her back in diapers."*

Avoiding the problem will only confuse your child; she won't learn to use the potty on her own. Frustrating as the problem may be, this is a good time to practice patience and tolerance—two essential parenting skills.

Instead, tell yourself,

> *"This too shall pass. I know my child will eventually*
> *learn to use the toilet when she needs to."*

Looking to the future helps you patiently accept your child's reluctance to use the potty without your reminders.

Talking to Your Child

Don't yell. Don't say,

> *"When I tell you to go potty, I mean it. Now get in there and go!"*

Being bossy might give you the impression that you can control your child's behavior, but it won't teach her how to listen and cooperate. You can control only your *reaction* to your child's behavior, not the behavior itself.

Instead, offer praise. Say,

> *"Thank you for sitting on the potty when I asked you to.*
> *Now you can stay dry, and I know you like feeling dry."*

Thanking your child for using the potty and reminding her that staying dry is important will encourage her to continue cooperating. Since she craves your approval, give her lots of praise when she cooperates.

Don't threaten. Don't say,

> *"If you don't go potty now, I'm going to get mad.*
> *You don't want me to get mad, do you?"*

Using anger to motivate your child's behavior will diminish her ability to empathize. You want her to care about others and treat them with respect; therefore, treat her as you would like her to treat you or anyone else.

Instead, practice. Say,

> *"Let's practice using the potty. Okay, let's walk from*
> *the kitchen to the bathroom. Now let's lift the toilet seat...."*

Practicing walking to the bathroom from various parts of your home can help motivate your child to stay dry. Encourage her to use the potty when she needs to and when you ask her to (before car trips, before bed, and so on).

Don't bribe. Don't say,

> *"If you'll use the potty, I'll give you some candy."*

Bribing your child tells her that she deserves a reward for cooperating.

Instead, make a deal. Say,

> *"I know you don't want to go potty right now,*
> *but when you've gone, then you can continue to play with your toys."*

Using Grandma's Rule helps motivate your child to take care of business before having fun, an important lesson for her to learn.

Don't label. Don't say,

> *"I give up. I'm sick and tired of your being so stubborn."*

Telling your child that she's stubborn sends her the hurtful message that she and her behavior are the same. Her behavior can change from appropriate to inappropriate; however, she's *always* worthy of your love regardless of how she behaves.

Instead, offer gentle reminders. Say,

> *"Check your pants. Are they dry? Doesn't dry feel good?"*

Having your child check her pants reminds her that she'd better go potty in order to keep herself dry.

Chapter Sixty

"Let Me Read to You."
"No! I Don't Want You to Read to Me!"

When you hear this protest, your first thought may be, "Oh no! My four-year-old will *never* like to read!" or, "He *has* to like being read to! *Every* child likes being read to!" Your child may not want you to read to him because he has trouble sitting still, he doesn't like the book you've chosen, he doesn't understand all the words, or he's focused on something else. Try to find the reason for his resistance whenever he says no to your invitation.

Helpful Hints

✋ Make reading to your child a part of your daily routine, so he learns to anticipate story time.

✋ Let your child see you reading by yourself each day. Being a good role model will motivate your child to want to read.

✋ Limit TV time and suggest reading when your child wants to be entertained.

✋ Avoid complaining about having to read the same book to your child every night. Children find comfort in repetition and consistency, so find ways to maintain your enthusiasm.

Self-Talk

Don't tell yourself,

"I hate the fact that he doesn't want me to read to him.
If he doesn't like to read, he'll never get into a good college."

Exaggerating the outcome of your child's resistance may make you overreact when he protests. "Hating" your child's refusal is a choice, as is "being intrigued" by it or "being curious" about it. Choosing a positive response will help you solve the problem.

Instead, tell yourself,

> **"Just because he doesn't want me to read to him
> now doesn't mean he won't want to read in the future."**

Remind yourself that your child's lack of interest in reading is temporary.

Don't tell yourself,

> **"I feel so hurt when he doesn't want me to read to him.
> I know he lets his father read to him."**

Don't take your child's rejection personally. When he rejects your offer to read to him, he's not rejecting you, just your suggestion.

Instead, tell yourself,

> **"I won't take it personally when my child doesn't want me to read to him."**

When your child refuses story time, keep in mind the long-term goals of instilling a love of reading, of spending time together, and of using your imagination. Doing so will help you cope with his refusal and will motivate you to keep reading to your child.

Don't tell yourself,

> **"He makes me so mad when he tells me he doesn't want me to read."**

Getting angry won't increase your child's interest in reading. His refusal is a neutral event; your reaction determines whether it's positive or negative.

Instead, tell yourself,

> **"I can handle this temporary setback in helping my child love to read."**

Affirming your ability to cope with your child's rejection leaves you open to finding solutions. When you stay calm, you send him the message that you respect his feelings and opinions even when they differ from yours.

Don't tell yourself,

> **"If he doesn't like reading, his teacher will think I'm a bad parent."**

Worrying about something you can't control, like a teacher's reaction, distracts you from helping your child enjoy story time.

Instead, tell yourself,

> **"I'm not going to worry about what others think.
> My job is to help my child learn to love reading."**

Focus on helping your child develop a lifelong love of reading, not on pleasing someone else.

Talking to Your Child

Don't overreact. Don't say,
"What's the matter with you? Why don't you want me to read to you?"
Don't suggest that there's something wrong with your child because he doesn't want to do something. Doing so teaches him that disagreeing with you is wrong. To make matters worse, asking a "why" question makes him have to defend himself.

Instead, invite feedback. Say,
"Help me understand the reasons why you don't want me to read to you."
Asking for feedback will give you valuable insight that will help you modify your approach and increase your child's receptivity.

Don't use guilt. Don't say,
"I took time out of my busy day to read to you, and now you don't want me to. What's the problem?"
Making your child feel guilty won't teach him to cooperate. It will only lead him to bottle up his feelings and distrust that you'll accept his honest sharing.

Instead, make a deal. Say,
"When we've read together until the timer rings, then you may play with your toys."
Respect your child's agenda while encouraging your own. You want reading time; he wants play time. Grandma's Rule allows your child to do what he wants *after* he's done what you've asked.

Don't demand. Don't say,
"Reading is important, and I'm going to read to you whether you like it or not."
Forcing your child to listen to you read won't instill a desire for reading. No one wants to be backed into a corner, so don't do it to your child.

Instead, be positive. Say,
"We had such fun reading this book last night, I thought it would be fun to read it again."
Reminding your child of how pleasant story time was in the past can motivate him to want you to read to him again. When you stay positive, your child will pick up on your enthusiasm.

SECTION X
HEALTH

Our greatest problems in life come not so
much from the situations we confront as from our
doubts about our ability to handle them.

—*Susan Taylor*

Chapter Sixty-one

"Please Put On Your Glasses."
"No! I Don't Wanna Wear Glasses!"

Who wants to put something on her face that falls down her nose, messes up her hair, and gets all smudgy when she touches them? Not a five-year-old! Glasses may be fashionable for adults, but for children, especially little ones, glasses often spell nothing but t-r-o-u-b-l-e. Keep your attitude positive and your compliments plentiful to motivate your child to see that glasses are her windows to the world.

Helpful Hints

👋 Make rules about when your child should wear glasses.

👋 Avoid complaining about wearing glasses or about their high cost. Your attitude is contagious.

👋 Compliment the glasses that others are wearing so your child sees that you think glasses are cool.

Self-Talk

Don't tell yourself,

"She's always complaining,
even about something as harmless as glasses."

Exaggerating your child's complaints with words like *always* makes her resistance more difficult to manage. She's complaining about the glasses, not everything.

Instead, tell yourself,

"I understand her reluctance to wear glasses.
I had to learn to like them, too, when I was her age."

Your empathy is valuable in teaching your child to accept wearing glasses. Helping her manage minor discomforts will increase her ability to tolerate major annoyances in the future.

Don't tell yourself,

"I don't care if she never wears her glasses. I'm too tired to fight about it."
Don't give up when it comes to your child's health and safety. Put her well-being above your inconvenience.

Instead, tell yourself,

*"Helping my child get accustomed to wearing
glasses is part of my parenting responsibility."*
Keep your child's needs in mind as you encourage her to wear her glasses. Remind her that she needs to wear them so she can see her world clearly and safely.

Talking to Your Child

Don't use guilt. Don't say,

"I paid a lot for those glasses, so you're going to wear them."
Don't expect that your child should do what you ask in order to make *you* feel good.

Instead, invite feedback. Say,

"Tell me what you don't like about your glasses."
Asking for your child's opinion can give you insight into her thinking and can help you develop a plan to encourage her cooperation. If she says, "They hurt my nose," you can adjust the nosepiece.

Don't scare your child. Don't say,

*"If you don't wear your glasses,
you'll fall down the stairs and hurt yourself."*
Predicting dire consequences for not following directions teaches your child to wear her glasses out of fear, not because it will help her navigate her world.

Instead, play a game. Say,

*"Let's see how long you can keep your glasses on.
I'll set the timer and you keep them on till it rings."*
Setting goals will help your child grow accustomed to wearing her glasses. Gradually increase the wearing time each day. Soon she'll have them on all day!

Don't ignore her feelings. Don't say,

> *"I don't care if the kids make fun of you. I don't want to hear about it."*

Your lack of empathy will destroy your child's desire to cooperate and will tell her that she's on her own. What a scary place the world would be without your support!

Instead, be positive. Say,

> *"I know you don't like wearing your glasses,*
> *but you can see things much better when you do."*

Pointing out the benefits of doing what you ask can help your child look beyond the temporary discomfort of getting used to glasses. Let her know that you're on her side.

Don't beg. Don't say,

> *"Please wear your glasses. Do it for Mommy!"*

Begging your child to cooperate will make her feel guilty when she doesn't want to do what you ask. Plus, it will teach her to beg to motivate others to cooperate.

Instead, remind her about the rule. Say,

> *"The rule says that you need to wear your glasses during the day."*

This helps your child understand that you're her ally with the common goal of following the rule.

Chapter Sixty-two

"Let's Put On Sunscreen." "No! I Don't Wanna Wear Sunscreen!"

To some five-year-olds, slathering on greasy, stinky sunscreen (or bug repellent) is a nightmare! Though your child may protest putting on sunscreen before going swimming or playing at the park, you'll be doing you both a favor by making sunscreen use a rule. Make sure to practice what you preach by letting your child put sunscreen on you.

Helpful Hints

🖑 Choose sunscreen (and bug repellent) that's effective and safe for young children.

🖑 Make rules about when and where your child needs to use sunscreen and/or bug repellent.

Self-Talk

Don't tell yourself,

"I hate his wriggling around while I'm trying to put sunscreen on him."
Telling yourself you hate your child's behavior will make you frustrated and angry and will stifle your ability to think creatively. It's much harder to cope when your mind is saying, "I hate," or, "I can't stand...."

Instead, tell yourself,

"I can handle a little resistance about sunscreen."
Your ability to cope depends on the self-talk you choose, so choose wisely. Telling yourself that you can cope with your child's refusal lets you do so.

Don't tell yourself,

"What will people think when my child is being so obstinate?"
Getting your child to cooperate involves no one but you and your child. Don't distract yourself by worrying about others' reactions.

Instead, tell yourself,

"My goal is to protect my child from the dangers of too much sun."

Remember why you told your child to put on sunscreen. His refusal to do so is a minor annoyance, not a source of embarrassment.

Talking to Your Child

Don't give in. Don't say,

"I'm tired of fighting with you about sunscreen.
If you get burned, maybe you'll learn."

Natural consequences are often effective motivators, but sometimes they're too dangerous to allow. This is one of those times. Telling your child that you don't care if he gets sunburned sends him the message that you don't care enough about him to enforce the rule.

Instead, remind him about the rule. Say,

"What's the rule about going out in the sun?"

Asking your child to tell you the rule not only reminds him of what you want him to do, it helps him internalize the behavior. Eventually, it will become a habit that doesn't require a reminder.

Don't threaten. Don't say,

"If you don't come over here this instant, I'm going to smack you."

Punishing your child for not cooperating will only increase his fear and anger; it won't motivate him to learn important lessons about staying safe. Threatening physical violence teaches him that might makes right—a harmful lesson.

Instead, ask questions. Say,

"Can you tell me why you don't like this sunscreen?"

When you understand your child's objections, you can resolve them to gain his cooperation. If he doesn't like the smell, you can buy something that's more appealing. This empathetic approach tells your child that you respect his feelings.

Don't bribe. Don't say,

> *"If you'll let me put sunscreen on you,*
> *I'll buy you a treat at the concession stand."*

Bribing teaches your child that cooperation comes at a price; it also teaches him that it's okay to manipulate others by "buying" their compliance.

Instead, make a deal. Say,

> *"When you have sunscreen on, then you may go in the pool."*

Grandma's Rule helps both of you compromise to meet your agendas—first yours, then your child's.

Don't use fear. Don't say,

> *"If you don't put sunscreen on, you'll get cancer!"*

Threatening dire consequences may motivate your child to do what you ask out of fear, but it won't teach him how to protect himself.

Instead, be positive. Say,

> *"We need to protect our skin from the sun so we don't get burned.*
> *When we use sunscreen, it keeps us safe and healthy."*

Focusing your child on taking care of himself helps him develop healthy habits.

Chapter Sixty-three

"It's Time to Go to the Doctor."
"No! I Don't Wanna Go to the Doctor!"

When we're unsure of what awaits us, experiences such as going to the doctor, dentist, or hospital are tantamount to jumping into a black hole. Try to remember what going to the doctor felt like to you as a kid, so you can understand how scary it is for your child. To maintain her trust, tell her the truth about what's going to happen (the doctor will look at her throat and ears, for example). Help her cope with any eventuality by talking about how you and she will be able to handle whatever happens at the doctor's office.

Helpful Hints

🖐 Select a doctor who uses kind language, lets you stay with your child, and relates well with children. Your insurance policy may limit your options, but do your best to find a healthcare provider who works well with children.

🖐 Talk to your child about *getting* to go to the doctor rather than *having* to go.

Self-Talk

Don't tell yourself,
"I get so embarrassed when my child screams at the doctor's office."
Feeling embarrassed will make it more difficult to help your child learn to cope. Remember, your child's behavior is telling you what she needs. Focus on that need, not on what others might be thinking about you.

Instead, tell yourself,
"I don't mind an occasional meltdown in the waiting room.
Other parents have probably experienced the same thing."
Telling yourself that meltdowns are no big deal helps you accept them as a normal part of life with toddlers and preschoolers. It also prevents you from worrying about others' opinions.

Don't tell yourself,
   "What's the matter with her? Going to the doctor isn't that bad."
Assuming there's something wrong with your child exaggerates the
problem and makes it unfixable. It also prevents you from helping her
cope with her fears.

Instead, tell yourself,
   "It's okay that she's afraid of doctor visits. A little caution is a good thing."
Acknowledging the advantages of caution increases your ability to
tolerate your child's wariness.

Talking to Your Child

Don't give in. Don't say,
   "You're so scared to go to the doctor, you're shaking.
   I'm going to cancel your appointment."
Avoiding fearful events won't help your child learn to cope with them.
In addition, it's irresponsible to risk her health because of your
well-intentioned efforts to protect her.

Instead, redirect her attention. Say,
   "I know you don't want to go, but the doctor helps you stay healthy.
   Let's think of fun things you can do at the doctor's office."
Focus your child on the books, toys, stickers, and other things she
enjoys at the doctor's office. Teaching your child to refocus will help
her cope with other unpleasant situations throughout her life.

Don't label. Don't say,
   "Don't be a baby! The doctor's not going to hurt you."
Calling your child a baby discounts her fears and teaches her that you
don't believe she can handle the challenge. These messages undermine
your effort to motivate her to cooperate.

Instead, ask questions. Say,
   "What don't you like about going to the doctor?"
Asking your child for her thoughts helps you understand her fears.
It also lets her know that you're empathizing with her and trying to
understand what's bothering her. Both can motivate her to cooperate.

Don't shame. Don't say,

> *"The doctor doesn't like children who aren't brave."*

Shaming your child teaches her that she's inadequate and unlikable because she's afraid. It also tells her that she is what she feels and that she can't become brave. Both are myths you don't want to create.

Instead, affirm her ability. Say,

> *"I understand that you don't want to go to the doctor,*
> *but you're brave and strong and I know you can handle it."*

Telling your child she's courageous and capable will lessen her fears and motivate her to cope with other frightening events.

Don't use guilt. Don't say,

> *"You've got to go to the doctor or you'll get really sick. Do it for me."*

Using guilt to motivate cooperation is a sure recipe for disaster. Your child will not only fear what might happen to her if she doesn't go, she'll fear losing your love and approval if she doesn't comply with your request.

Instead, change the focus. Say,

> *"When we're through with your checkup,*
> *then we'll have lunch at Grandma's. She always loves to see you."*

Looking beyond the immediate task to a pleasant event that will follow can help your child overcome her fears.

Chapter Sixty-four

"It's Time to Take Your Medicine." "No! I Don't Wanna Take My Medicine!"

You know your child's medicine smells bad, looks bad, and by all accounts tastes bad. What do you do? You may be tempted to lie to him and say it's yummy and fun to take, but you're better off minimizing his suffering by offering flavorful drinks or licks of candy between swallows. Being part of the solution puts you on your child's side, and cooperation is a byproduct of that happy alliance.

Helpful Hints

🖐 Always try to put yourself in your child's shoes to understand how he feels, and remember to provide plenty of hugs with the medicine.

🖐 Check with your pharmacist to find out if your child's medicine comes in a tasty flavor or in a form that's easier to take.

🖐 Avoid complaining about taking your own medicine.

🖐 If your child has difficulty swallowing medicine or gags when trying to swallow, make it more palatable by mixing it with food (if medically appropriate), by using a special spoon, by making a game out of taking it, or by using an oral syringe. Talk to your doctor or pharmacist if you have any questions about how your child should take the medicine.

Self-Talk

Don't tell yourself,
"I'm not going to force him to take something he doesn't like."
Refusing to follow your doctor's treatment could jeopardize your child's health and make a habit of medical noncompliance that could threaten your child's life.

Instead, tell yourself,

"My job is to help my child follow the doctor's orders."

Keep your child's health and safety in mind as you teach him to cope with adversity.

Don't tell yourself,

**"He's going to take his medicine if I have
to hold him and pour it down his throat."**

Using force won't help your child learn to cooperate. Instead, it will convince him that aggression is an acceptable way to get someone's cooperation. Taking medicine is unpleasant enough for children. Don't add to the nastiness by using force.

Instead, tell yourself,

**"I don't want my child to have to take nasty medicine,
but I know a little discomfort is necessary sometimes."**

Of course you want to protect your child from suffering, but being a responsible parent means helping your child cope with life's hardships.

Talking to Your Child

Don't tattle. Don't say,

"Do you want me to tell the doctor you won't take your medicine?"

Threatening to tattle will make your child fear the doctor.

Instead, make it a game. Say,

**"I know you don't like the taste of the medicine,
but it's important for you to take it. Let's do it on three.
Ready? One, two, three, down it goes."**

Reinforce the importance of taking the medicine, and make it fun to take. This will motivate your child with the promise of fun and your attention—a priceless combination!

Don't threaten. Don't say,

"If you spit the medicine back out, I'll slap you. Now swallow it."

Threatening your child with physical violence may achieve results in the short term, but it will teach him that might makes right. In addition, knowing that he has no control over the situation will make him feel helpless.

Instead, make a deal. Say,

**"When you've swallowed the medicine,
then you may have a drink of milk."**

Grandma's Rule helps your child learn to tolerate unpleasantness and delay gratification. Knowing he'll get to replace the nasty taste with something good helps him feel more in control.

Don't threaten to take away privileges. Don't say,

"If you don't take your medicine, you can't watch TV today."

Taking away your child's TV privileges won't help him learn to cooperate so he can take care of himself. It will only set the stage for a battle when he wants to watch TV.

Instead, focus on the positive. Say,

**"This medicine is going to help you get well.
Every time you take it, you'll feel better."**

Stressing the important link between medicine and health—and using the power of suggestion—will help your child be more cooperative. He'll also learn that he can help keep himself healthy.

Don't belittle. Don't say,

"You know better than that. Now take your medicine."

Implying that your child's stupidity is preventing his cooperation creates three problems: It makes him upset that you think he's stupid, it makes him feel bad about himself, and it makes him further resist taking his medicine.

Instead, affirm your child. Say,

**"I'm sorry you don't like the medicine,
but you're brave and strong and I know you can swallow it."**

Affirming your child's strength and bravery helps him want to prove to you and himself that he has these qualities. He wins and you win: The medicine goes down and his self-image goes up.

Chapter Sixty-five

"You Need to Get a Shot."
"No! I Don't Wanna Get a Shot!"

Do you remember your childhood fears when you knew you were going to get a shot or stitches? Keep them in mind as you can calmly and lovingly respond to your child's protests. Although she may not have a choice in the matter, you can empathize with her fears as you encourage and reassure her. In addition, request that your child's doctor or nurse apply a topical anesthetic to numb the skin before giving a shot. The belief that pain builds character is false. The latest research has shown that physical pain in infancy can make children overreact to shots and other painful procedures later.[9]

Helpful Hints

- If possible, choose a doctor or nurse who handles these procedures well and who's good with children.

- Avoid telling your child horror stories about when you got shots or stitches, but be honest with her about how getting them feels. You don't want to compromise her trust by telling her the procedure doesn't hurt.

- Check with your doctor about providing fun distractions while your child is getting a shot or stitches. For example, have your child blow bubbles with a bubble wand during the procedure.

Self-Talk

Don't tell yourself,

*"It's my fault that she needs stitches.
I should have been watching her more closely."*

Blaming yourself for your child's accident will distract you from helping her cope with her fear of getting stitches.

Instead, tell yourself,

> *"I don't like to see my child uncomfortable,*
> *but sometimes it's unavoidable. My job is to help her cope."*

Understanding that minor discomforts are sometimes necessary to avoid greater suffering will help you remain calm while you reassure your child.

Don't tell yourself,

> *"Watching my child get a shot makes me sick. I can't be there for her."*

Reinforcing your own fear of needles ensures that you won't be able to help your child when she needs you most. It also models running away from challenges.

Instead, tell yourself,

> *"I need to overcome my own fear of*
> *shots to help my child cope with hers."*

Remind yourself that most of the pain is in the anticipation rather than the shot.

Don't tell yourself,

> *"This is so terrible! I can't let my child suffer."*

Exaggerating your child's discomfort will increase your anguish and prevent you from doing what you need to do for her health. Refusing the shot is not in anyone's best interest.

Instead, tell yourself,

> *"Helping my child cope with getting a*
> *shot is my responsibility as a parent."*

Your job is to help your child handle her fears, to comfort her, and to reassure her that you're there for her.

Talking to Your Child

Don't use guilt. Don't say,

> *"Do it for Mommy."*

Using guilt will teach your child to do tasks only to make you happy or to prevent your displeasure. She should cooperate because she wants to improve her health, not because she wants to avoid hurting your feelings.

Instead, stay positive. Say,

**"I know you don't want to get a shot,
but it's very important to keep you healthy."**

Focus your child on the benefits of getting the shot or stitches.

Don't use putdowns. Don't say,

"Don't be a wuss like your daddy."

When you criticize your child's other parent, you force your little one to choose sides. She'll think, "I don't want to be like Daddy!" and she'll cooperate just to stay on your good side.

Instead, compliment. Say,

**"I know you're brave and strong and can
handle getting a shot to stay healthy."**

Affirming your child's bravery and strength will encourage her to overcome her fear.

Don't lie. Don't say,

"Shots don't hurt. I don't know why you're making such a fuss."

Lying to your child and discounting her fears mean double trouble: You're undermining her trust in you, and you're telling her you don't care about her fears.

Instead, be honest. Say,

**"I know that shots hurt a little, but they don't last long. Let's blow
bubbles while you get the shot, and you'll feel better in a jiffy."**

Lovingly acknowledge what your child is going through. Your emotional and physical support will help her believe that you'll always tell the truth and always be there when she needs you.

> If you are a parent, recognize that
> it is the most important calling and rewarding
> challenge you have. What you do every day, what
> you say and how you act, will do more to shape
> the future of America than any other factor.
> —*Marion Wright Edelman*

Appendix

Milestones of Development

The following chart describes some of the milestones parents can expect their one- to five-year-olds to reach during their preschool years. These milestones are presented according to the age at which they usually occur. Since each child develops on an individual timetable, a particular child may be ahead of, on, or behind the statistical average. Consult your child's healthcare professional if your child is consistently delayed in reaching milestones or if you're concerned about other aspects of your child's development.

Age	Milestones
1–2 Years	• Explores his environment; gets into things • Takes one long nap a day • Plays alone for short periods of time • Explores his body
2–3 Years	• Runs, climbs, pushes, pulls; is very active • Legs appear knock-kneed • Feeds himself with fingers, spoon, and cup • Can remove some of his clothing • Explores his genitalia • Sleeps less, wakes easily • Likes routines • Becomes upset if his mother is away overnight • Wants to do things himself • Is balky and indecisive; changes his mind • Has flashes of temper; changes his moods often • Imitates adults • Plays beside but not with children his own age • Is not yet able to share, wait, take turns, give in • Likes water play • Prolongs the good-night ritual • Uses single words, short sentences • Is often negative; says "no" • Understands more than he can say

3–4 Years
- Runs, jumps, and climbs
- Feeds himself; drinks neatly from a cup
- Carries things without spilling
- Can help dress and undress himself
- May not sleep at naptime, but plays quietly
- Is responsive to adults; wants approval
- Is sensitive to expressions of disapproval
- Cooperates; likes to run simple errands
- Is at a "Me, too!" stage; wants to be included
- Is curious about things and people
- Is imaginative; may fear the dark, animals
- May have an imaginary companion
- May get out of bed at night
- Is talkative; uses short sentences
- Can wait his turn; has a little patience
- Can take some responsibility, such as putting away toys
- Plays well alone, but group play can be stormy
- Is attached to parent of opposite sex
- Is jealous, especially of a new baby
- Demonstrates guilt feelings
- Releases emotional insecurity by whining, crying, requesting reassurance of love
- Releases tension by thumb sucking, nail biting

4–5 Years	• Continues to gain weight and height
	• Continues to gain coordination
	• Has good eating, sleeping, and elimination habits
	• Is very active
	• Starts things, but doesn't necessarily finish them
	• Is bossy, boastful
	• Plays with others, but is self-assertive
	• Has short-lived quarrels
	• Speaks clearly; is a great talker
	• Tells stories; exaggerates
	• Uses toilet words in a silly way
	• Makes up meaningless words with lots of syllables
	• Laughs, giggles
	• Dawdles
	• Washes when told
	• Is at the "How?" and "Why?" stage
	• Demonstrates dependence on peers

References

1. Gottman, John. *Raising an Emotionally Intelligent child*, Fireside, 1997.

2. Haidt, Jonathan. "The Emotional Dog and its Rational Tail: A Social Intuitionist Approach to Moral Judgment," *Psychological Review*, Volume 108, Number 4, (October 2001): 814–34.

3. Fredrickson, Barbara. "Cultivating Positive Emotions to Optimize Health and Well-Being," *Prevention and Treatment*, Volume 3, Article 1, (2000).

4. Ibid.

5. Ropeik, David and George Gray. *Risk: A Practical Guide for Deciding What's Really Safe and What's Really Dangerous in the World Around You*, Mariner Books, 2002.

6. American Academy of Pediatrics. "Children, Adolescents, and Television," *Pediatrics*, Volume 107, Number 2, (February 2001): 423–26.

7. Ibid.

8. Becque, M. D., et al. "Coronary Risk Incidence of Obese Adolescents: Reduction by Exercise Plus Diet Intervention," *Pediatrics*, Volume 81, Number 5, (1988): 605–12.

9. Schechter, Neil. *Pain in Infants, Children and Adolescents*, 2nd Edition, Lippincott, Williams, and Wilkins, 2002.

Index

A

Activities
  encouraging practice for, 159–61
  going to lessons and, 31–3
  sports practices and, 34–7
  swimming lessons, 41–4
Airplane travel, 19–22
Anger
  child's helpfulness and, 186, 187
  departure procedure and, 3
  diaper changes and, 129
  dressing and, 51, 58
  fixing hair and, 144
  getting into the car and, 9
  getting out of the bathtub and, 120
  holding hands in the store and, 24
  independent play and, 98
  interest in reading and, 208
  playing quietly and, 105
  putting on pajamas and, 165
  tooth brushing and, 122
  visits to grandparents in nursing home and, 197
  wearing shoes and, 54
Appearance, parent focusing attention on, 35
Asking child questions. *See* Feedback from child
Authoritarian approach
  bullying child into swimming lessons, 43
  demanding child go to preschool, 148
  forcing child to listen to read, 209
  harm from, 133
  going to lessons and, 31
  misusing, 12
  sleeping in a big bed and, 171
  telling child where to sit and, 85

B

Baby
  giving child's room to, 178–81
  playing quietly during naps of, 103–5
Babysitters, 182–4
Bathroom, going to, 204–6
Bathtub, getting out of, 118–20
Bedtime. *See* Sleep
Begging
  changing clothes and, 61
  changing to a new room and, 180
  choosing what to wear and, 58
  getting out of the car and, 14
  sharing toys and, 108
  wearing clean clothes and, 48
  wearing glasses and, 214
Belittlement
  babysitters and, 184
  being quiet for baby and, 104
  carrying child and, 199
  changing clothes and, 60
  fixing hair and, 144
  getting dressed and, 51, 57
  going to home of ex-spouse and, 39
  phone conversations with ex-spouse and, 89
  taking medicine and, 223
  using a quiet voice and, 83

using comfort items and, 193
  See also Name-calling; Putdowns; Shaming
Blame placed on child,
  going to daycare and, 30
  harm of, 11
Blame placed on ex-spouse
  daycare and, 28
  sleeping in own bed and, 175
Blame placed on parent
  child's feelings and fears and, 17, 20, 42
  talking to ex-spouse on phone and, 88
  thumb sucking and, 202
  time-outs and, 188–9
Blowing the nose, 139–41
Bossing, holding hands and, 26
  See also Authoritarian approach
Bribery
  airplane travel and, 22
  carrying child and, 200
  changes to a new room and, 180
  cleaning up toys and, 117
  defined, xvi
  departure procedure and, 5
  diaper changes and, 129
  getting dressed and, 51
  getting into the car and, 8
  getting out of the car and, 15
  getting out of the bathtub and, 120
  going to a new preschool and, 152
  going to daycare and, 30
  going to lessons and, 33
  going to preschool and, 149
  going to the potty and, 206
  going to sports practice and, 37
  hair washing and, 138
  holding hands in the store and, 25
  playing music loudly and, 111
  playing quietly and, 105
  putting on shoes and, 55
  sitting in the car seat and, 12
  sleeping in own bed and, 174
  staying at the table and, 66
  sunscreen use and, 217
  swimming lessons and, 43
  table manners and, 69
  thumb sucking and, 203
  using a quiet voice and, 82
  using comfort items and, 193
  using the elevator/escalator and, 18
  visits to grandparents in nursing home and, 197
  where to sit and, 86
Brushing and combing hair, 142–4
Bullying, swimming lessons and, 43
  See also Authoritarian approach

C

Car travel
  getting into, 6–9
  getting out of, 13
  helpful hints for, 10, 13
  sitting in car seat and, 10–2
Carrying child, 198–200
Change, adjusting to

problem; Guilt, parental; Positive attitude; Role modeling; Self-talk; Support, parental

Phone conversations, 87–90

Picking up toys, 114–7

Play(ing)
computer/video games, 99–102
independent, 95–8
loud music and, 109–11
quietly, 103–5
sharing and, 106–8

Police officers, 12

Positive attitude
airplane travel and, 22
babysitters and, 184
changes to a new room and, 179, 180
getting into the car and, 6, 7
getting out of the car and, 14
going to preschool and, 149
haircuts and, 126
putting on shoes and, 54
reading and, 209
time-outs and, 190
using the elevator/escalator and, 18
wearing glasses and, 214

Positive consequences
departure procedure and, 5
getting into the car and, 9
getting shots and, 226
preschool and, 158
taking medicine and, 223

Potty, going to the, 204–6

Practice
encouraging, 159–61
going to daycare and, 27
going to the potty and, 206
holding hands in the store and, 25
putting on shoes and, 55
sports, 34–7
talking to ex-spouse on the phone and, 90
use of manners and, 79
using a quiet voice and, 82

Praise
babysitters and, 184
changing to a new preschool and, 151
changing to a new room and, 181
child walking independently and, 200
child's helpfulness and, 186, 187
going to daycare and, 29
going to the potty and, 205
hand washing and, 132
holding hands while shopping and, 26
playing computer/video games and, 101
playing quietly and, 105
practicing for activities and, 161
preschool room assignments and, 158
sitting in the car seat and, 12
sleeping in the big bed and, 172
staying at the table and, 66
use of manners and, 69, 79
using a quiet voice and, 83
wiping the nose and, 141
See also Support, parental

Preschool
going to a new, 150–2
listening to teacher at, 153–5
not wanting to go to lessons and, 146–9

room assignments in, 156–8

Privileges, taking away, 223

Promises, keeping, 172

Punishment
holding hands in the store and, 25
independent play and, 97
playing music loudly and, 111
putting pajamas on and, 166
See also Time-outs

Putdowns
airplane travel and, 21
changes to a new room and, 180
getting out of the car and, 15
getting shots and, 226
holding hands while shopping and, 25
sharing and, 107
table manners and, 69
tooth brushing and, 123
using comfort items and, 194
See also Belittlement; Name-calling; Labels

Q

Questions, asking child. See Feedback from child

Quiet time
naps and, 168
while baby is sleeping, 103–5

R

Reading to child, 207–9

Respect, 153

Rewards. See Bribery

Role modeling, xv
airplane travel and, 21
blowing nose, 139
exercising calm and self-controled behavior, 171, 189
footwear and, 53
getting shots, 225
good manners, 77
helpfulness, 185
kindness, 195
leadership skills, 125
playing music loudly and, 109
reading and, 207
sharing TV choices, 76

Rules
bathtub, 120
bedtime, 173
car seat sitting and, 12
carrying child and, 198
changing clothes, 59, 60
cleaning up toys and, 114, 116
getting dressed and, 52, 57, 58, 59
going to home of ex-spouse, 39
going to preschool and, 149
hair needs, 143
hand washing and, 130, 132
holding hands in the store and, 24
manner, 77
naps and, 169
playing music loudly and, 109, 111
playing quietly and, 103
practicing for activities and, 161
putting pajamas on and, 164, 166
school room assignments and, 157
sharing and, 106, 107
sleeping in own bed and, 174

hair washing and, 138
listening to teachers and, 155
school room assignments and, 157
sharing and, 108
swimming lessons and, 44
table manners and, 69
talking to ex-spouse on the phone and, 90
Swimming lessons, 41–4

T

Table manners, 67–9
Tattling
    departure procedure and, 4
    taking medicine and, 222
    TV viewing and, 94
Teachers
    interviewing, 31
    listening to, 153–5
Teaching flexibility, 175
Teaching how to blow the nose, 141
Teasing, 181
Television
    battles over, 74–6
    helpful hints for viewing, 92
    taking away privileges of, 223
    turning off, 92–4
Thank-you, saying, 77–9
Threats
    babysitters and, 184
    changing clothes and, 61
    child's lack of helpfulness and, 186
    cleaning up toys and, 116
    departure procedure and, 4
    diaper changes and, 128
    getting dressed and, 50
    getting into the car and, 7, 8
    getting out of the bathtub and, 119
    getting out of the car and, 15
    going to daycare and, 28
    going to lessons and, 32
    going to preschool and, 149
    going to the potty and, 206
    hand washing and, 132
    holding hands in the store and, 24
    independent play and, 97
    listening to teachers and, 154
    nail cutting and, 135
    naps and, 168
    negative consequences of, xvii
    phone conversations with ex-spouse and, 90
    playing computer/video games and, 101
    playing music loudly and, 110
    putting pajamas on and, 165
    sharing and, 108
    sitting in the car seat and, 12
    sleeping in own bed and, 174
    sports practices and, 36
    staying at the table and, 66
    table manners and, 68
    taking medicine and, 222, 223
    thumb sucking and, 202
    time-outs and, 190
    TV viewing and, 94
    use of manners and, 79
    using comfort items, 192–3
    using the elevator/escalator and, 18

wanting to wear dirty clothes and, 47
wearing shoes and, 54
wearing sunscreen and, 216
where to sit and, 86
wiping the nose and, 141
Three to four year olds, 228
Thumb sucking, 201–3
Time-outs
    hand washing and, 132
    playing computer/video games and, 102
    playing music loudly and, 111
    resisting, 188–90
    sharing toys and, 108
Timer game
    changing clothes and, 61
    cleaning up toys and, 116
    getting dressed and, 50
    getting out of the bathtub and, 119
    getting pajamas on and, 166
    independent play and, 97
    playing computer/video games and, 101
    playing quietly and, 105
    practicing for activities and, 161
    sharing toys and, 108
    staying at the dinner table and, 64
    wearing glasses and, 213
Tooth brushing, 121–3
Toys
    cleaning up, 114–7
    sharing, 106–8
Transitions. *See* Change, adjusting to
Travel
    airplane, 19–21
    See also Car travel
TV *See* Television
Two to three year olds, 227

U

Ultimatums, 21

V

Video games, 99–102

W

Washing hair, 136–8
Washing hands, 130–2
Wearing glasses, 212–4
Whining
    departure procedure and, 4
    hand washing and, 131
Wiping the nose, 139–41

Y

Yelling, 205
    See also Anger

Also from Meadowbrook Press

Discipline without Shouting or Spanking
The most practical guide to discipline available, this newly revised book provides proven methods for handling the 37 most common forms of childhood misbehavior, from temper tantrums to sibling rivalry.

Look Who's Talking!
Help your child learn to communicate by enhancing language development. Using the latest academic research, Laura Dyer, MCD, has written the most comprehensive book available that shows parents how to enhance their children's language development, starting at birth.

Practical Parenting Tips
This best-selling collection of helpful hints for parents of babies and small children contains 1,500 parent-tested tips for dealing with everything from diaper rash, nighttime crying, and toilet training to temper tantrums and traveling with tots. Parents will save time, trouble, and money.

365 Toddler Tips
This book gives parents of toddlers 365 ways to meet everyday challenges. Routines such as "Monster Check" and "Boo-Boo Bunny" are sure to become classics in your home. Along with Penny Warner's help and guidance, you'll also find anecdotes from other parents of toddlers.

Busy Books
The Toddler's Busy Book, *The Preschooler's Busy Book*, *The Children's Busy Book*, and *The Arts and Crafts Busy Book* each contain 365 activities (one for each day of the year) children can do using items found around the home. The books offer parents and caregivers fun ideas that stimulate a child's natural curiosity and creativity and channel a child's energy.

**We offer many more titles written to delight, inform, and entertain.
To order books with a credit card or browse our full
selection of titles, visit our website at:**

www.meadowbrookpress.com

or call toll-free to place an order, request a free catalog, or ask a question:

1-800-338-2232

Meadowbrook Press • 5451 Smetana Drive • Minnetonka, MN • 55343